MICHAEL TOBERT grew up in Nottinghamshire, an English county famous for Robin Hood, D.H. Lawrence, coal mines and just about nothing else. He rather liked it. His happiest days were spent communing with nature, a predilection that led him to find employment on a pig farm. The onset of adolescent vegetarianism, however, prompted a change of tack and, after Oxford University, he tried his hand in the City of London (where he hated every moment), at a water company in the West Midlands and at the London Business School. He then headed north where his fragmented career culminated in an attempt to start his own publishing company. This, to his wife's astonishment, was not a total failure. He has lived in St Andrews for the last 20 years and spends his spare time on the golf course. By dint of constant practice, he is sometimes able to break 80. He is a member of the R&A and has three children. This is his first book.

D0208872

Pilgrims in the Rough

St Andrews beyond the 19th hole

MICHAEL TOBERT

Luath Press Limited

EDINBURGH

www.luath.co.uk

First published 2000
Reprinted 2001

The paper used in this book is recyclable. It is made from low chlorine
pulps produced in a low energy, low-emission manner
from renewable forests.

Printed and bound by
J W Arrowsmith Ltd., Bristol

Typeset in 10.5 point Sabon by
S. Fairgrieve, Edinburgh

Maps by Jim Lewis

The author's moral right has been asserted.

A Cataloguing-in-Publication Data record for this book is available
from the British Library.

To Tessa, who, because of this book, has spent too many days lying dejectedly on the carpet when she should have been out playing golf – but has seen fit to forgive me

Contents

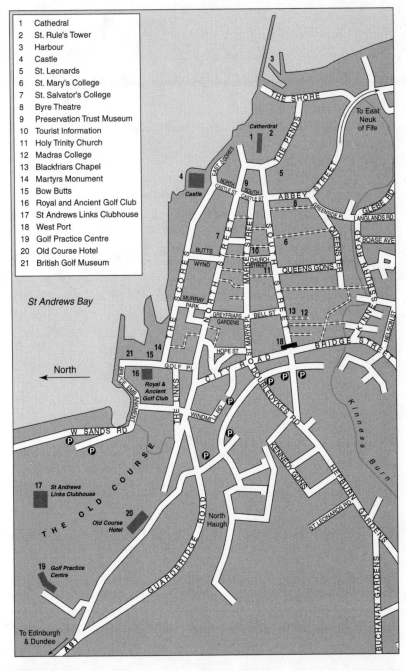

1	Cathedral
2	St. Rule's Tower
3	Harbour
4	Castle
5	St. Leonards
6	St. Mary's College
7	St. Salvator's College
8	Byre Theatre
9	Preservation Trust Museum
10	Tourist Information
11	Holy Trinity Church
12	Madras College
13	Blackfriars Chapel
14	Martyrs Monument
15	Bow Butts
16	Royal and Ancient Golf Club
17	St Andrews Links Clubhouse
18	West Port
19	Golf Practice Centre
20	Old Course Hotel
21	British Golf Museum

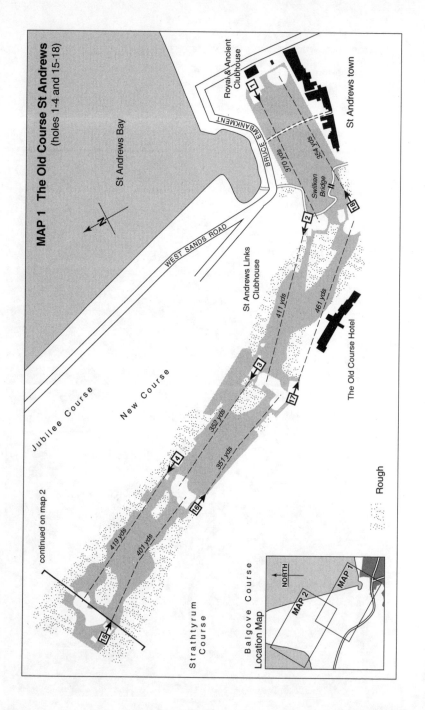

MAP 1 The Old Course St Andrews
(holes 1-4 and 15-18)

St Andrews Bay

Royal & Ancient Clubhouse

St Andrews town

1

Swilken Bridge

18

354 yds

370 yds

BRUCE EMBANKMENT

2

411 yds

461 yds

WEST SANDS ROAD

St Andrews Links Clubhouse

The Old Course Hotel

Jubilee Course

New Course

3

17

352 yds

351 yds

continued on map 2

4

16

419 yds

401 yds

15

Strathtyrum Course

Rough

Balgove Course
Location Map

NORTH

MAP 2

MAP 1

IO

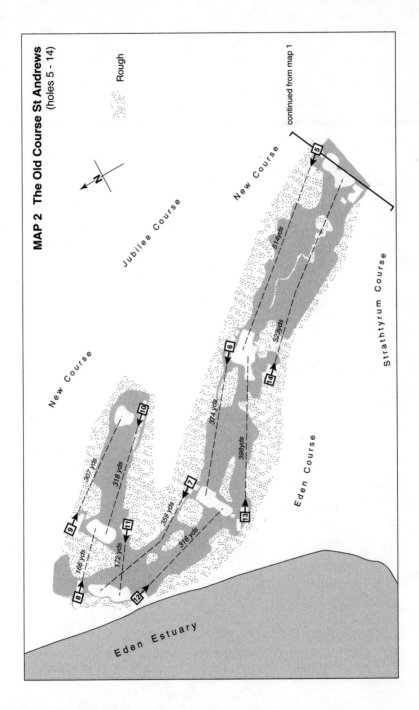

MAP 2 The Old Course St Andrews
(holes 5 - 14)

Rough

Jubilee Course

New Course

New Course

Strathtyrum Course

Eden Course

Eden Estuary

continued from map 1

514yds

523yds

374yds

398yds

307yds

318yds

359yds

316yds

166yds

172yds

5

6

14

7

13

9

10

11

8

12

II

Acknowledgements

TO MY FAMILY, OF COURSE, for putting up with me. To David and Deborah Douglas, whose comments, as the book was in progress, were amusing, encouraging, honest and apposite. To Jurek Pütter for putting me straight on a number of points and sharing with me some wonderful tit-bits about medieval St Andrews. To Dr Peter Lewis of the British Golf Museum, and Dr Barbara Crawford of the Department of Medieval History, St Andrews University, for casting an expert eye over the text. (All errors are, needless to say, the responsibility of the author.) To Duncan McAra, without whose drive this book would still be mouldering in my bottom drawer. And especially to Madeleine, my in-house editor-in-chief, who was always ready to abandon her homework when the need arose.

I am particularly indebted to Jurek Pütter for his original illustrations on pages 26, 32, 60, 84 94, 112, 126, 134, 142, 152, 154 and 166, and for permission to extract details from his previously published works on pages 35, 54, 97, 115 as well as on the front cover. Grateful thanks also to Simon Weller for his original drawings on pages 68, 82 and 88. 'The Man who Missed the Ball on the First Tee at St Andrews' by H.M. Bateman is reproduced on page 62 by kind permission of the Royal and Ancient Golf Club of St Andrews.

Preface

MIRACLES DO HAPPEN. In 1978, a company in Dundee momentarily took leave of its senses and offered me a job. I had been married for three weeks when I broke the news that it was all change: Scotland here we come. Linda, my bride, was not amused. For her, mum, dad, brothers, aunts, uncles, cousins, the entire known world existed south of Hadrian's Wall. I had phoned her from a telephone box by the Tay Bridge at six o'clock in the morning to tell her how marvellous Dundee was. Did I actually say that? About Dundee? Apparently I did – and that she should start packing.

We drove north the following weekend in the 2CV to try to find somewhere to live. No sooner had we passed Jedburgh than it started to rain. Actually, that's putting it mildly. It bucketed down. Cats and dogs trampolined on our permeable leatherette roof. Noah was seen floating by in a loch off the A697. My attempt to soften up my reluctant bride by a quiet summer's wandering through the Borders was not working out as planned, and arriving in Dundee didn't improve matters either. Twenty years ago, Dundee and urban renewal were concepts that had yet to become acquainted. It was dilapidated, it was impoverished, it was the place the BBC chose when they wanted a stand-in for Moscow. Besides which, every pub, against whose frosted glass windows we poked our drenched and dripping noses, looked as if you had to have been drinking there since birth to stand a sporting chance of coming out alive. I could see my better half's upper lip begin to tremble in a courageous, but clearly doomed, attempt to persuade herself that the words 'I do', which she had haltingly enunciated so recently, were not a terrible mistake. 'What about a look at St Andrews,' I said cheerfully. 'I can always commute.' And so it came to pass that we drove over the Tay Bridge, and, as we entered this hallowed town, the sun broke through the clouds and smiled upon us. We have been here ever since, without a backward glance.

Living in St Andrews, however, privilege though it is, does not by itself remove those festering sores that we all have and are inclined, from time to time, to scratch. The sore in question is that I have always wanted to write a travel book. I like travel. I like exotic places. I like my holiday expenses to be tax-deductible. Yet somehow, I hadn't written one. Life had got in the way, and the intent had stayed on the back burner. That is until 18 July 1998, which began as any other July day (with a promise that today I would definitely cut the grass) and ended with the realisation that two magnificent travel stories were waiting for me on my doorstep: one that starts as you walk around the old medieval streets of St Andrews; and the other as you stand on the first tee of the Old Course with 18 uncertain holes ahead of you. Life could carry on and, though I might not come back with a suntan, the old sore could be scratched. I talked this over with Madeleine (no. 2 daughter), and she thought it was a great idea. Madeleine is very encouraging at moments of decision. So that's it. A travel book about St Andrews. A book that combines the game I love and the course I have played for 20 years with the town that I consider as close to paradise as I am likely to find this side of the pearly gates.

Introduction

An Extremely Brief History

ST ANDREWS IS WITHIN spitting distance of the Arctic Circle. It is north of Moscow and on the same line of latitude as Hudson's Bay in Canada. If it weren't for the fact that we are on an island, and that the Gulf Stream has not yet been entirely obliterated by global warming, St Andrews would be the home of ice hockey rather than the Home of Golf. It is 50 miles north of Edinburgh, in what used to be the Kingdom of Fife, and not on the way to anywhere. The A91 reaches St Andrews and stops, just as the Trans-Siberian Railway reaches Vladivostok and stops. If you are here, the presumption is that you are not just passing through.

St Andrews goes back a long way. Natives have been living in these parts since the days when mankind was still in short trousers, but recorded history didn't really get going until the Romans reached the river Tay in AD 79.[1] I have to say that Romans this far north were a surprise. I had been brought up to believe, quite wrongly, that they never conquered Scotland because they didn't have socks. You certainly never see pictures of them wearing anything other than a pair of open-toed sandals which (visitors please note) is not recommended footwear for this part of the world. They must have been a hardy lot because they stuck it out until AD 300, by which time the lure of the Tuscan sunshine had clearly become irresistible. The only thing the Romans left behind in St Andrews itself was one worn coin dated AD 268 which was found in the grounds of St Leonards School.[2]

Next up were the Picts, who painted themselves with a blue dye called woad and hence acquired their name which means 'the painted people'. On the whole the use of woad has died out in Scotland, except when supporters assemble to watch the national team play football. The Picts were heathens, which meant that they were suitable targets for any Christian missionary who happened along but, this being the Dark Ages, the surrounding gloom makes it hard to know which set of missionaries earned the bonus points – perhaps St Columba's team on Iona, perhaps St Ninian's from Whithorn in Dumfries and Galloway, or perhaps St Cuthbert's from Lindisfarne in Northumbria.[3] Also arriving under cover of night was the mysterious St Rule who, as legend has it, landed here bearing the bones of St Andrew, the Apostle. It is after these dry bones that St Andrews is named. By the 10th century, or thereabouts, and thanks in part to Viking preferences for rape and pillage holidays on the west coast,* St Andrews had become the HQ of the Scottish Church.[4]

Visitors to St Andrews, even those with eyes only for golf, can hardly fail to notice the spectacular ruins at the east end of town. I suppose some might. I do know a Canadian who was so taken with the golf courses that it was years before he realised that the town had an east end, but for most of us, addicts included, the remains are more or less unmissable. They belong to the great Cathedral, founded in 1160. By the time it was consecrated in 1318 (an event which prompted Robert Bruce to ride his horse up the main aisle), it was the largest church in the country, and indeed the largest building erected in Scotland until the Victorians developed a taste for railway stations on the grand scale. It was built in the days when what mattered was religion. It put St Andrews in pole position, it kept the big-spending clergymen in town, and it did wonders for tourism. Yet by 1559, it was in ruins. The town spent 150 years putting the thing up, used it for a further 240 years, and then, egged on by John Knox (of whom more later), laid it to waste. To get a fix on the scale of self-mutilation involved, imagine the townsfolk of today taking a tractor and ploughing up the Old Course.

The old town of St Andrews grew up around the Cathedral, with South Street and North Street sweeping up to the Cathedral gates. Both streets are broad and elegant, in spite of breaking da Vinci's rule that a street should be as wide as the height of the

---

* Iona, the original centre of the Scottish church, was persistently raided. In 849, some of St Columba's relics were moved east to Dunkeld.

houses. They are several times wider, which is just as well or where would we all park our cars. The medieval street plan was, and is, delightfully simple. Think of an egg lying on its side. The Cathedral is at the pointy east end and from it South Street and North Street make up the sides of the shell. Down the middle of the egg, through the yolk as it were, runs Market Street. To the north (ie beyond North Street) is a street called The Scores, and then the North Sea. To the south and west are the modern additions to the town. The golf courses begin on the north-west end of the egg. Everything is walkable, and there isn't anyone, I don't care how bad his sense of direction, who will find it possible to get lost.

With the Cathedral came the University. Religion and learning are old bedfellows. Founded in 1410, the university is the oldest in Scotland and preceded in Britain only by Oxford and Cambridge. Over the years it has churned out some great names, the movers and shakers in Scottish history, as well as in the wider world, martyrs, scholars, swordsmen, scientists, poets, you name it. Even Marat, the French revolutionary, took an MD in medicine here, but that was in the days when standards were lower and before he had discovered the perils of letting young ladies into his bathroom. If you are in St Andrews on the first Saturday after the students come back in April, you can see many of the great names of St Andrews life walking through the town in the Kate Kennedy procession. St Andrew himself leads the way carrying the X-shaped cross that appears on the Scottish flag (and on extras in *Braveheart*), whilst John Cleese, a former Rector, brings up the rear.*

There were tourists in St Andrews long before golfers, only in the old days they were called pilgrims. Curious as it may seem, indeed as it was, nowhere else in Northern Europe boasted the relics of an apostle like St Andrew, so those in need of salvation – a sizeable market in any age – risked plague, wars, bandits and our usual weather of 'winds with gales' to get here. The Vatican Office for International Pilgrimage, a sort of medieval travel bureau,

---

* John Cleese, and indeed St Andrew, are impersonated by students.

rated St Andrews the second most important pilgrimage site in North-Western Europe (after Santiago de Compostella in Spain).[5] Penitent pilgrims poured in from Italy, Bohemia, Poland, France and Flanders. From the north, Scandinavians filtered down via the Cathedral of St Magnus in Orkney. In response, St Andrews' second oldest profession (its bed-and-breakfast ladies) put up their prices, thus initiating a tradition which continues today: if you want a room in Open week, start saving early.

It never does to underestimate the speed with which things can turn sour. Take the world economy. One moment we are told that because of free trade and new technology, we will all continue to grow richer and richer until the last trumpet. Then there is a little local difficulty with the Thai Baht and a stumble or two from the Russian President, and alarm bells about world recession start ringing. It is the same on the golf course. One par follows routinely after another, oh what an easy game golf is, and then there is a freakish bounce, the ball lodges against the face of a bunker and you end up taking eight. This is more or less how it was for St Andrews. By the 16th century, things could not have been going better. The tourist trade was booming. Up to 300 ships from the Continent would sail into harbour for the big town fair in April. The Church had more money to spend than the State[6] and spent a good proportion of it right here in St Andrews. The town boasted 60 to 70 bakers,[7] and a brewer on every street corner to provide the clerics, the pilgrims and the merchants with their evening tipple. A fine old time was being had by all, and then along came the Reformation, John Knox with his vitriol against 'idolatrie' and Catholic excesses, and all that nonsense with the Cathedral.

Quite apart from anything else, when your major assets are some ancient bones and the regional HQ of a corporation as wealthy as the Catholic Church, it doesn't make sense to declare publicly that bone worship is so much mumbo-jumbo and to reduce the Cathedral to a pile of old stones. It is like McDonald's telling the world that junk food is bad for your health and then bulldozing all their burger joints. It just doesn't demonstrate much of an eye for business. Anyway, when the tourists had stopped coming, and the Old Church, with its insatiable appetite for the finer things in life, had been kicked out, all the juicy handouts stopped with them. No more queues of people outside the butcher, the baker and the candlestick maker. No more endless streams of pilgrims willing to pay through the nose for a place to lay their troubled and unworthy heads.

The sacking of the Cathedral in 1559 was not quite the end of St Andrews, but almost. The Archbishops, now Protestant, managed to cling on with some interruptions until 1689, at which point bishops of all denominations were deemed unnecessary – but by then St Andrews was staring into the abyss. Trade had collapsed, business was moving to the larger cities, and Union with England and the opening up of the US colonies would drag the centre of gravity southward and westward. St Andrews' central position in Scottish affairs was at an end and it wasn't long before the buildings were crumbling and the people were leaving in droves. Dr Johnson, the dictionary man, came to St Andrews in 1773, and muttered about 'indigence and gloomy depopulation'.[8] (Johnson was not the most neutral observer, mind you. One of his other lines was that 'the noblest prospect which a Scotchman ever sees is the high road that leads to England'.) By 1800, there were no more than two or three ships in the harbour (a 99% decline), a dozen bakers (an 83% decline), and two brewers[9] – and when anything falls by that much, it is time for the financiers to climb out onto the window ledge and jump off. By 1876, numbers at the University had evaporated to a mere 130[10] which was fine for a drinks party, but a little thin for an enduring place of scholarship. The prospects were looking bad. Worse than bad – terminal. The town was slaloming, accelerando, down the slippery slope, and the only thing that saved it from going splat into its own medieval paving stones was the little white ball.

Golf and St Andrews have been joined at the hip for centuries. Even at its dawn, golf began to dominate waking hours to such an extent that James II of Scotland had to ban it (in 1457) because it interfered with the small matter of defence against the English. Not enough practice hours were being put in on the longbow which, with the auld enemy lurking, showed either commendable sang froid or major league masochism. 'It's the English, it's the English', came the cry. 'Aye, weel, A'm twa oop on wee Jamie and A'm nay daunderin hame.' It wasn't just the commoners who played. They were all at it, even royalty. Mary Queen of Scots was seen out on the Links* a few days after the tragic loss of her husband, Darnley, giving rise to speculation that she had a tee time booked and didn't dare cancel it. James VI of Scotland, when he went to London in 1603 to become James I of England, took his clubs with him.[11] The precise date that golf came to St Andrews is not known, but it is thought to have been played here by 1400. It was certainly in full swing before 1552, when Archbishop Hamilton agreed – in exchange for being able to keep the rabbits that roamed the course – to confirm the town's right to play golf (and football) on the Links. The things a man will do for rabbit stew. By 1691, St Andrews was described as 'the metropolis of golfing'.[12]

The first stirrings of organisation in the game began in the middle of the 18th century. The Honourable Company of Edinburgh Golfers gathered together in 1744 to play for a silver golf club and drew up golf's first set of 13 succinct rules, the most delphic of which was rule 2, 'Your tee must be on the ground'. As opposed to what? On your caddie's head? Ten years later, in 1754, it was the turn of the Royal and Ancient Golf Club of St Andrews.† Now the R&A had one great advantage over the other emerging golf clubs. At a time when the Honourable Company and others were moving from course to course, the R&A had its own great Links. The early Opens, when not at Prestwick or Musselburgh, were played at St Andrews. The great players of the day, such as Allan Robertson, Tom Morris, or Andra Kirkaldy, worked as caddies

---

* This incidentally is the earliest known reference to a woman playing golf. The date was 1568. The Links in question were the fields of Seton (east of Edinburgh).

† The R&A actually started life as the Society of St Andrews Golfers and stayed that way until 1834 when William IV gave it his royal blessing.

or clubmakers in the town, or like Willie and Mungo Park, came here for the big money matches. The R&A was royal, it was ancient and it played on God's own links in a town where golf had become the only game in town. So it was that when the senior clubs wished in 1897 to create a uniform code of rules, it was decided unanimously to give the job to the R&A.

It was only a short step from there to becoming the ruling body of world golf. OK, the United States has decided to go its own way (the Declaration of Independence has a great deal to answer for), but that still leaves the other ninety-nine countries who look to the R&A to tell them what the rule is if they play an air shot over somebody else's ball, or whether they can replay without penalty if, as actually happened, an earthquake measuring 7.1 on the Richter scale erupts at the top of their backswing and causes them to drive out of bounds.[13] Not that the R&A always gets it right. A journalist telephoned to ask if the stymie* had been abolished. By mistake, he was put through to the lady behind the bar who told him in no uncertain terms that it had not. 'There is a bottle on the shelf and we still serve it!'[14]

As for the Old Course itself, which has witnessed the development of the game from its very beginnings, seen all the champions and hosted many great Open Championships, it has become the most renowned piece of golfing turf on the planet. The pilgrims are back and the town is again as vibrant and cosmopolitan as it was all those hundreds of years ago.

---

* A stymie is where your opponent's ball lies between you and the hole requiring you to play round (or over) it. The stymie was abolished in 1952. Players now have to lift and mark. For an amusing and informative trot through the rules of golf, John Glover's *Celebration of 100 years of the Rules of Play* (whence come the earthquake and stymie incidents) is highly recommended.

Travels Around
The Town

CHAPTER I

The Mound behind the R&A

IT'S YOUR FIRST MORNING in St Andrews. The plane was delayed, British Airways decided that one of your bags should be re-routed via Amsterdam, and you didn't get to your hotel until late last night. A couple of whiskies, perhaps, to settle the stomach, and then to bed. You tottered down this morning, ate more Scottish breakfast (porridge, kipper or eggs and bacon, toast and tea) than was good for you, and here you are staggering out of your hotel. My advice would be to head for the sea. If you are staying on The Scores or in the B&Bs in Murray Park or North Street, you can probably smell it. Follow your nose. Go to the front across The Scores and take a deep breath. It is wonderful stuff, sea air from St Andrews. If ever air deserved to be bottled, this does. Breathe in a jug-full. When you feel up to it, turn your head gently to the left and there you will see a bandstand below a sloping grassy bank. If the sun is out, lie on the bank, close your eyes and imagine one of our school bands murdering the Radetsky March. A scattering of adoring parents and uncommitted passers-by are sitting where you are, beaming in pleasure or grimacing in pain depending on their blood ties to the participants. Those that are grimacing in pleasure have the mixed emotion that comes from being both related and musical. On a hot Sunday in summer, reclining on the pristine grass as the heady cocktail of melody, cacophony and sea breeze swirls around you, is one of St Andrews' finer indulgences.

The area around the bandstand is redolent with history. The truncated obelisk behind the bandstand, that looks like Cleopatra's Needle after my wife has washed it, is the Martyrs Memorial, commemorating the town's burnt Protestant martyrs (to whom, we will return). Close by is Witch Hill, where the Protestants got their own back by burning the witches, which they continued to do, on and off, for the best part of 150 years. When the Statutes against witchcraft were repealed in 1736, many St Andrews Presbyterians were outraged.[15] Witch Lake, in the waters below (to the right), was where witches took their heads-I-win, tails-you-lose test. Putative witches splashed down here after being flung from the cliff above. If they swam, they were witches and were burnt. If they drowned, they demonstrated their innocence. Since left thumb was tied to right big toe and right thumb to left toe (to replicate the cross), a lady would have had to be something out of the ordinary to stay afloat. Yet some did – perhaps with a sort of convulsive tortoise-like backstroke – because they were then taken away for firewood.

All this does make you wonder what sort of place St Andrews must have been in those days. The odd aberration may be excusable, but anything that lasts 150 years, which is six generations give or take, shows attachment. My guess is that a town that can wax lyrical about the pleasures of making a bonfire out of some helpless old crone will probably come down quite heavily on the weird and wonderful, and on all those little oddities that make life worth living. But that was then and part of growing up perhaps. Nowadays, the town is a gentle, slightly academic, tolerant sort of place, where people are decent to their kids, oddballs can survive and prosper, and just about everybody, witch or not, can walk around the town secure in the knowledge that they are most unlikely to be burnt, knifed, mugged or otherwise impeded.

Next to Witch Lake, on the R&A side, is what remains of the grand outdoor swimming pool called the Step Rock which was 300 feet long and ran from the beach out to the sea. When it was built in 1903 it was for men only, partly because the tradition was for men to swim naked. Women were allowed in in the 1930s, which either boosted swimwear sales, or the birth rate. Between 1930 and 1960, the 'Steppie', as it was generally known, was packed on hot days, with deckchairs, refreshment kiosks doing a roaring trade, and massed ranks of the local population lounging on the concrete platform in front of the diving board and water chute. Old photographs of those days, when the sun shone and the people looked contented, evoke a gentler age. The popularity of the Steppie started to wane in the 1960s and, today, the only things swimming there are a family of seals, courtesy of the Sea Life Centre.

Now that the Steppie is no more, there is always the West Sands, the long beach that runs parallel to the golf courses. Nothing is better for washing away the cares of the day than a plunge into the North Sea on a warm summer's evening when there is scarcely a ripple on the water or another soul in sight. The water is on the arctic side of bracing, but the sands slope so gently that you have plenty of time to acclimatise. This makes getting in up to the lower thigh relatively easy. It's the next bit that sorts the men from the boys. A quick *allee oop* is recommended. Otherwise, the thought of ice water inching over vital parts is too terrifying to contemplate.

If a swim in the great outdoors is not to your taste, you can always go for an indoor dip in the East Sands Leisure Centre (which is to your right if you are looking out to sea, and round beyond the harbour). I should perhaps here sound a word of warning. When it was built, the Council had visions of erecting a tropical paradise on the east coast of Scotland. The pool was shaped like an enticing Caribbean lagoon, with a gently sloping entry to replicate the golden sands of St Vincent. Alongside the pool and reaching to the ceiling was a palm tree, imported at great expense, with its refulgent leaves stretching over the heavily chlorinated waters below. Unfortunately, three problems with this municipal dream were to surface within weeks of opening. First, the palm tree died. Either chlorine fumes were not to its taste, or it needed fresh air. The Council solved the problem to its satisfaction by attaching plastic palm leaves to the top of the trunk where the original leaves once were, but this did leave some unanswered questions in the minds of the swimmers as to why a tree, presumed dead, had suddenly sprouted verdant new foliage overnight. The second problem was that the pool was not very large, certainly not that part of it that was deep enough for swimming, and the tropical paradise was usually so packed that it was difficult to do more than stand up. The third problem, associated with the second, was that the changing area tended to flood. People came out of the pool and dripped over the floor so that, by about 10.30 in the morning, the changing area took on the appearance of Venice's Piazza San Marco at high tide (without the orchestras). In order to get into your trousers without soaking them, you had to stand on a bench and, since this took your head above the height of the changing cubicle and forced you to look straight into the eyes of the person (male or female) in the next cubicle, who was also fumbling about down below, you didn't half feel like a prat. A sort of giraffe-esque prat.

My last suggestion for a swim is the outdoor pool at the Castle Sands underneath the Castle Rock and within hailing distance of St Rule's cave. (This was the cave where old St Rule was said to have lived after bringing the Apostle's bones to St Andrews.) Two-thirds of my offspring swim there, Madeleine with her friends, and Andrew (occasionally). They recommend it. The crabs don't bother them a bit. Alternatively you might say, particularly if you have come from the warm waters of the South of France or Florida, that perhaps the swim can wait until you get back home.

Above the Step Rock Pool and towards the R&A is the Bow Butts, which was a sort of driving range for archers. Archery started off as military service. A man had to learn to shoot. If he didn't show up at the butts six times a year, the King's sheriff was instructed to 'mulct him of a wether'. Don't ask. Women, or more particularly that women's libber supreme, Mary Queen of Scots, were also known to have drawn a bow. Years ahead of her time was Mary. And, of course, with everyone being urged to fire off, accidents did happen. James Melville, in his *Diary*, tells how in 1592 a Mr John Caldcleuch, a master in theology, was practising in the garden of St Mary's College when he missed not only the target, but also a number of thatched cottages beyond it and 'winged in the neck an auld honest man, a maltman of the town, who had the ill luck to be passing through the adjoining wynd.'[16] Ill luck indeed. It must be quite a shock to be walking along, minding your own business, and find an arrow plunging into the back of your neck. The maltman's pals were, not surprisingly, outraged. They broke into the College and threatened to burn it down; a threat happily unfulfilled. When the nation's army stopped fighting with bows and arrows, archery became sport. The top competition in St Andrews was the Silver Arrow, a University two-day event, which started in 1618 and came to an end in 1754. There was a town drummer and a piper to announce the start of the contest and a parade of archers, in their traditional costumes, through the streets. The winner was piped back to William Geddes' tavern for junketing.[17] The whole thing was strictly amateur, and mainly for the rich and titled. The winner was not only not paid for winning, but also had to bequeath a silver medal to hang on the university arrow. This took more out of the wallet than a round of drinks.

The Bow Butts is the approximate spot where, in days gone by, the first hole of the Old Course was thought to have begun.* Archers would lay down their bows and take up their clubs. A fearsome drive over the R&A Clubhouse, you might say, and what did the members make of balls flying past the front door as they left the club after their traditional seven course lunch washed down by a pint or two of claret? The answer is that in those days the R&A clubhouse had not migrated to its present site, rather than that the members were too drunk to notice, although they may well have been, had the balls indeed whistled by.

This part of town is not a bad spot for a first sighting of the prospect to the west: the sweep of the West Sands, the Links themselves, the new visitors clubhouse, and the public lavatory in the foreground, crafted in concrete, which was put there in order to block a splendid view of the sea that would otherwise greet visitors turning off North Street and into Golf Place. It can't be moved because there is some sort of pumping station underneath. And to the east is the shore leading round to the Castle, the Cathedral and the harbour.

---

* At least some people think that. Others believe it started more or less where it starts now. Unless an ancient map is magically brought to light, I don't suppose we will ever know.

CHAPTER 2

The Cathedral

IT WAS ONLY AFTER I had lived here for a number of years that it dawned on me that the ruins at the end of South Street are not just the remains of a Cathedral, but of a whole complex of religious buildings: the 11th-century St Rule's Church; a 13th-century Augustinian priory; a great precinct wall which runs around the whole site; and outside it the Culdean Church of St Mary on the Rock. If the whole thing were being built today, I have no doubt that Fife Council would call it a Religion Centre to go alongside the Town's Technology Centre, Leisure Centre and Gateway Centre. Just about the only part of town that doesn't have a Centre is its middle.

Celtic Christianity came to St Andrews (or Kilrimont as it was then called) during the Dark Ages. There was a monastic community here in the middle years of the 8th century, when Oengus (Angus) was King of the Picts. By the 10th century, Roman ways were gaining ground. In the reign of Culen, son of Indulf (966 to 971), Bishop Cellach II is said to have been 'the first to go to Rome for confirmation', along with two gentlemen about whom we know nothing except for their splendidly invertebrate names, Leot and Sluagadach.[18] The last bishop to bear a Celtic name, Fothad II, died in 1093,[19] after which the clergy contented themselves with mundane appellations like Robert and Arnold, which don't have quite the same mysterious ring to them. Before he departed this earth, Fothad had built the new church* that came to be known as St Rule, whose tall, square tower still stands to this day.

Given what happened in 1559, it is remarkable that the tower is still in one piece and upright. Unless you claim a disability allowance, have a pacemaker or are eight months pregnant, you

---

* The precise date of the building of St Rule is unclear. Some, or all, of it may have been built after Fothad's time between 1130 and 1150.

have to climb it. A narrow and winding stone staircase opens out at the top from where you can feast your eyes on the most magnificent vista that St Andrews has to offer. Laid out before you is a bird's-eye view of the old medieval town (plus its less aesthetic modern additions), the West Sands, St Andrews Bay and the rolling farmland of Fife. Not to be missed. The locals, it has to be said, rarely make the effort, but you will meet other tourists on the climb and the occasional student who has gone up for one last windswept cigarette before Finals.

No sooner had St Rule's Church been built than the clerics decided it wasn't up to scratch. They wanted something bigger, something grander, something more appropriate to their wealth, their status and their central position in the Scottish Church. So, in the great tradition, they decided to erect a huge cathedral, just as in the 19th century, the burghers of every industrial city from Glasgow south would build ever more splendid town halls.* The Cathedral was begun in 1160 when religion was what made the world go around and when the faith in Scotland, as in the western world, was unhesitatingly Catholic. It grew up with the Church of Rome, and it came to an end as a living entity when the Protestants cast Catholicism out of Scotland. What remains of it are sundry truncated walls and its two imposing ends that somehow gloriously defy the laws of gravity and establish the dimensions of the magnificent building it once was.

The public, noisy, smelly and dirty part of the Cathedral was the nave at the western (town) end. This was where the students of St Leonards College gathered when they wanted a blether,[20] and where the pilgrims, having dragged themselves across continents without benefit of bath soap, congregated. The east end held the high altar, various chapels, the tombs of many of the bishops and, most important of all, the relics of St Andrew himself, on which the local tourist industry depended. St Andrew had been generous, reputedly donating 'three fingers of his right hand, the arm

* This sort of lavish over-the-top expenditure went out of fashion in the 20th century, except in Brussels. Notwithstanding the Millennium Dome, it rather grates against the British sense of propriety but, then again, if governments were not prepared to spend taxpayers' money like water, what would future generations have to marvel at.

The medieval Cathedral, foreshortened, as the town might have seen it in 1525.

bone that hangs down from the shoulder, one tooth and a kneecap.'[21] Astonishingly, nobody in the Middle Ages seemed to doubt that they were the genuine article. The fact that the only place in Northern Europe to have the substantial relics of an apostle should be up here on the extreme edge of the known world, did not seem to occasion even so much as a raised eyebrow, despite holes in the evidence through which any prosecution lawyer worth his salt could drive a coach, horses, and half the English army.

The legend of St Andrew comes in several versions, which doesn't do much to inspire confidence, but the one inscribed on our kitchen tea towel includes many of the essential ingredients. A monk named St Rule (or St Regulus) had a vision in which he was commanded to lay his hands on as many of St Andrew's bones as he could carry and sail to the 'north-west ends of the earth'. Wherever his ship was wrecked, and it turned out to be right here (around AD 350), was to be St Andrew's resting place. Many years later, the Kings of the Picts and Scots were in great danger from an advancing army of Saxons. The night before the battle, the Kings and their armies awoke to see two bright shafts of light forming a St Andrew's cross against the dark blue sky. The next day a great victory was won, and the St Andrew's cross has been carried into battle by the Scots ever since. That the legend depends entirely on a monk who was nine-tenths mythical and on a meteorological event that would astonish the forecasters at the Met Office, is neither here nor there. The fact is that the Scots believed that St Andrew had chosen them, and the rest of the world concurred.* When you are a small country wracked by internal division and battling against a much larger enemy, the idea that someone has reached down from the heavens and tapped you on the shoulder, does wonders for self-confidence.†

* In 1301, during the Wars of Independence against England, the Scots tried to persuade Pope Boniface VIII to take their side. They argued successfully that since St Andrew was the brother of St Peter, the Pope as St Peter's successor should safeguard the independence of St Andrew's chosen people, the Scots. In the 14th century this argument made sense.

† In 1320, with Bruce pressing to have his sovereignty recognised, Scotland produced its first independence manifesto, the wonderfully stirring and historically inaccurate Declaration of Arbroath. In the preamble, Scotland is described as blessed by Christ and protected by St Andrew.

Cautionary Tale (1)

On the subject of credibility and saints, there is a story in *Scotichronicon*, a 15th-century history by the eminent Fife cleric, Walter Bower (1385-1449), about two beggars in the town of Tours (France). One beggar was blind, the other crippled, and they had struck up a business partnership. The blind man carried the cripple, and the cripple told him where to walk. This image of mutual support touched the hearts of the passers-by, and the partnership made a good deal of money. Now the local saint was St Martin, who had a reputation for curing invalids, and the beggars got wind of plans to take the Saint's body around the town in procession, on a route that went past their house. This was alarming news because an inadvertent cure would mean that plans for flotation on the Tours Stock Exchange would have to be called off. They decided to scarper, if this is appropriate terminology for a blind man carrying a cripple – but let us allow Bower to take up the story. 'While they were moving away,' says the good Abbot, 'they unexpectedly encountered Martin's body directly, and because God bestows many benefits upon those reluctant to receive them, both men against their wishes were immediately healed, although they were extremely annoyed as a result'.[22] Indeed.

St Andrew, as the main man (deceased) in town, had many processions in his honour. These were great local occasions. The Cathedral would be packed with townsfolk and pilgrims who, when the sermonising was done, would spill out into the sunshine* and follow bishop, clergy and saintly bones around the streets of the old town. The route taken was probably the loop down South Street and back along North Street, which would leave the booths and stalls in Market Street undisturbed and able to prepare for the festivities to follow.[23] In the medieval world, Saints' Days meant party time. Days off work. Festivities. So much so that, on one memorable occasion in 1335,[24] John de Strivelyn, an English knight who was in the middle of a siege of Lochleven castle, decided that rather than hang about all day doing boring siege-stuff, he and some of his men would join the feast day of St Margaret at

---

* It was always sunny in the old days.

Dunfermline.* While he was away, the Scots slipped out of the castle and broke the siege, which no doubt left John de Strivelyn with some explaining to do.

The Cathedral was never cut out for a mellow old age. In the 1270s, after a hundred years of constant clutter from scaffolding, large carts and be-cheeked masons, the Cathedral was just about finished when the west end blew down in a gale. No sooner had they recovered from that than, in 1304, Edward I of England, up here for the siege of Stirling (and a round at Gleneagles perhaps), found himself short of ammunition and decided to help himself to the lead on the Cathedral roof. In 1378, twenty years after its inauguration, a great fire damaged the choir and transepts.[25] And then came John Knox. Now to be fair, John Knox did not just appear. There were harbingers. There were preceding events. The Catholic clergy had been setting a less than perfect example for some time. They lived too well. They sold too many indulgences. Criticism had already begun to seep out of the woodwork when, in 1517, Luther nailed his famous list of 95 complaints against Rome to his church door in Wittenberg. Over the next few years, much of Northern Europe, including England, became Protestant. Scotland made some efforts to hold back the tide by introducing a range of ultra-sensitive measures to encourage adherence to the old faith – such as declaring that eating meat during Lent was punishable by death[26] – but, strangely enough, such inducements did not have the desired effect.

Nor did the burning of Protestant heretics. Patrick Hamilton went up in smoke in 1528 (outside St Salvator's Chapel in North Street). He wasn't the first heretic to burn in Scotland, but he was the first known Scot and a great grandson of James II to boot.[27] It took him six hours to die and 'his reek infected all it blew upon'. Henry Forrest was put on trial in the Cathedral in 1533 and burnt

* This, at least, was how Walter Bower reported it. The idea of English soldiers, involved in rape, pillage and whatever else English soldiers of the day got up to, taking time off for a shopping trip sounds, by today's standards, improbable. However, as long as the soldiers didn't go round sounding too obviously English (not, by the way, recommended behaviour in Dunfermline, even today), then who's to object?

so that the flames could be seen on the other side of the Firth of Tay. Next was George Wishart in 1546, and finally, in 1558, Walter Myln, aged 82 and past the age when a man should have to account for his opinions. Myln was the last heretic to be tried in the Cathedral and incidentally was able to provide a final testament to the excellent acoustics of the place. Having struggled up into the rostrum, an eyewitness recalls that he spoke with vigour and 'made the church to ring and sound again'.[28] None of this did more than prepare the stage for Mr Knox.

John Knox was endowed with the flowing beard of an Old Testament prophet, a voice compared to 'five hundred trumpets continually blustering in our ears,'[29] views on women which would sound alarming even to the politically incorrect, and an unshakeable belief in his own rectitude. A sort of early day Ian Paisley, only more so. He began preaching in the town church of St Andrews, Holy Trinity, on 11 June 1559 and continued to blast away until the 14th with, I assume, some minor allowance made along the way for bodily functions. As soon as he had finished orating, the mob (Knox's henchmen and local townsfolk) no doubt driven crazy by earache and desperate for fresh air and exercise, headed for the Cathedral and wrecked the place. The *Historie of the Estate of Scotland* says that 'the sermon was scarcely downe, when they fell to work to purge the kirk and break down the alters and images and all kind of idolatrie . . . and before the sun wes downe there wes never inch standing bot bare walls.'[30] This was probably an exaggeration, but it certainly didn't take long to shift just about everything that wasn't nailed down. The plate, the valuables, the bells, the brass, the timber, the lead, all went, and it was not only the common man who had his snout in the trough. The Lords and clergy were in there with the best of them. The tombs of the bishops were raided, and the gold and silver, jewels and rings spirited away. The things that were 'attached', like the walls, took a little longer to shift, but in the end more was taken than remained. The Cathedral became the town quarry, and a sadder end is hard to imagine. Dr Johnson summed up the whole sorry state of affairs as well as anybody. 'Well', he said, 'that Knox had set on a mob, without knowing where it would end; and that, differing from a man in doctrine, was no reason why you should pull down his house about his ears.'[31]

A year after the sacking of 1559, Catholicism was out across Scotland and the Protestants were in. This didn't do much for the job prospects of the Catholic priesthood, as you may imagine. Undeterred, however, they sniffed the wind, and did what all careerists up and down the generations have done. They jumped ship. The higher up the pecking order they were, the further they jumped. Take the case of John Winram, sub-Prior of the Cathedral Priory. To the old Catholic hierarchy, he had been a loyal servant, indeed a prominent prosecutor of heretics. When 1559 came round, he declared undying allegiance to the new faith and secured for his troubles the plum appointment of Superintendent of Fife.[32] A contemporary, the parson of Ballingry, summoning all his powers of reserve, described him as a 'fals, dissaitful, gredy and dissimblit smayk', which needs no translation (but in case you are struggling with 'smayk', it means rogue). By virtue of such flexibility, Winram was able to keep his house and job, and indeed appears to have made enough out of selling the Cathedral silver and Priory lands to have given his nephews and stepsons plenty to squabble over when he died. His tombstone is to be found in St Leonard's College Chapel and there is a street named after him in town. Such are the rewards of pragmatism. Winram wasn't the only one with his eye on the main chance. His boss, the Prior James Stewart, was as bad. When the appointed hour arrived, Stewart declared himself for the Protestant cause and earned his crust through unscrupulous property deals. Whether he retained his former mistress, who had lived and dined with him in the Priory and was known to his colleagues as the 'Lady Venus', is not clear.[33]

Butting on to the south side of the Cathedral are the remains of the Augustinian Priory. The Priory provided the staff quarters for the Cathedral, and occupied the space around the grassy square marked 'cloister'. The dreadful red sandstone that you will see is the 'restoration' undertaken by the Marquess of Bute in the 1890s. He used red sandstone because – and one can only applaud his integrity – he didn't want anyone to confuse the restoration with the original – an ambition he achieved completely. The incongruous mixing of old and new produces the same sort of feeling you would get if you looked at a Rembrandt that had been touched up by a house painter. Into Bute's handiwork has now been inserted a shop, where you can buy a token to go up St Rule's tower, useful guides to the Cathedral, books on Scottish history, T-shirts, pencils and assorted tourist bric-à-brac. It is where we bought our tea towel. Next door is an attached building that has the feel of a cellar, except that it isn't underground, and was the only part of the Priory that had the luxury of a fireplace. It is now a museum of stones from Scotland's and the Cathedral's past: carved stones, inscribed stones, tombstones, stones that have seen better days. The best stone of the lot is the St Andrews sarcophagus, which contained the relics of a Pictish king, possibly Constantine, son of Fergus, who died in 820.[34] It is beautifully carved. One of the details seems to portray a large bird attempting either to eat, or impregnate, a decent-sized horse – but what do I know? Anyway, you should go and see for yourself. If you want further background on the Cathedral, drop in on Jurek Pütter, a graphic artist and historian who has spent his working life painstakingly reconstructing medieval St Andrews. His drawings are wonderfully detailed accounts of the town's golden age (1460–1560) and, for a modest remuneration, he will sell you a print of the old place and provide as much background as you can handle.* What St Andrews could also do with is a virtual reality show that would take us back 500 years, let us walk around the Cathedral columns, sit on the pews, gaze down the aisle and touch the relics. Anybody out there with £2m in loose change?

Around the whole Cathedral site is almost a mile of 16th-century stone wall, built on even earlier 14th-century walls. The still visible coat of arms of the builder (Prior John Hepburn) carries his motto *ad vitam*, a punchy little exhortation which has been adopted by the neighbouring private boarding school, St Leonards. The school would have their pupils believe that *ad vitam* is an encouragement to seek out life, to grab life with both hands. In fact, the full quote is *ad vitam, aut culpam*,[35] which

* Jurek Pütter's contact details are listed in the section entitled 'Useful Addresses'.

means 'for life or until found out', but that's not a message to hammer home to formative young minds. They'll find out soon enough anyway. There are various towers along the wall, and the largest looking north to the sea is the haunted tower. It had been sealed up for years until opened secretly in 1868. Inside, amongst a pile of bones, was – some say – the perfectly preserved body of a young lady wearing white leather gloves.

The Ghosts of St Andrews

There is no shortage of ghosts and ghouls in the Auld Toun: the phantom coach of Archbishop Sharp, with its four large, black horses that travels the Strathkinness road in silence; the murdered Prior who, on moonlit nights, can be seen looking over the Tower of St Rule; the monk who beckons strangers into the tunnels and staircases under the medieval Cathedral; and many more. Such stories are the preserve of one of St Andrews' more colourful characters, Dean of Guild, William. T. Linskill, 1855–1929 (deceased).* Here is a fragment of a report to him on the 'Lady of the Haunted Tower'.

'It must have been the end of January or the beginning of February, and I was strolling along to the Kirkhill after dinner and enjoying the fine evening and the keen sea breeze, and thinking about the old, old days of the Castle and Cathedral, of Beaton's ghost, and many other queer tales, when a female figure glided past me. She was in a long, flowing white dress, and had her beautiful dark hair hanging down past her waist. I was very much astonished to see a girl dressed in such a manner wandering about alone at such an hour, and I followed her along for several yards, when lo! just after she had passed the turret light she completely vanished near the square tower in the Abbey Wall . . .'

If you like this kind of thing, buy the book[36] or go on the Witches Tour that runs from the Tudor Inn in North Street most weeks and after dark in winter. It will take you through the back passages of the old town and is entertainment for the whole family.

* Linskill had two lucky breaks in life. His first was that he was taught to play golf by young Tommy Morris, the finest golfer of his day. That alone would have been enough for most of us. His second was that he jumped off the seven o'clock train as it was leaving Leuchars Station for Dundee. The date was 28 December 1879. Twenty minutes later, as the train was crossing the river Tay, the bridge collapsed in high winds, causing the death of 75 men, women and children, with the engine, five carriages and the brakevan of the North British Railway Company lost in the waters below.

Don't leave the Cathedral without looking at the eloquent Morris memorial (by the Cathedral wall on the south side). Young Tom Morris' wife died in childbirth in September 1875, and young Tom himself was dead by Christmas of, it is said, a broken heart. He was twenty-five years old and the winner of four Open Championships. Old Tom, who also won four, died in 1908 after falling down the stairs of his Golf Club. He outlived his son by twenty-three years. No one has been held in higher regard in these parts than Old Tom. You might also like to notice, by the Cathedral gate at the town end, a lone urn standing on a plinth. Its isolation is total, like a beautiful girl who has swum out to a distant rock to sunbathe and been stranded by the receding tide. How the urn – perfect for winter bulbs or as a classy addition to the allotment – survived the looting and carnage which destroyed so much of everything around it, I cannot imagine. Yet no one made off with it or smashed it to a pulp. I like to believe, and this is fanciful I know, that it was rescued by a kindly soul and looked after until such time as it could be safely returned.

Golfers in the Graveyard

I would hazard a guess – in fact I would put money on it – that from the dead buried in St Andrews Cathedral you could pick a golf team that would beat any team from any other graveyard in the world. The skipper would be Allan Robertson, the finest golfer of his generation: the man who, in 1842, was prevented from playing in a competition because the other competitors, Tom Morris among them, thought they would have no chance if he took part[37] – which is rather like telling Tiger Woods not to turn up for the Masters. The Morrises, with their eight Opens between them (in 1861, '62, '64, '67, '68, '69, '70 and '72) would make the team, as would the other St Andrews' men who won the Open: Andrew Strath who won the Championship in 1865 and died of tuberculosis three years later; Tom Kidd (1873); Bob Martin (1876, 1885); Jamie Anderson (1877-9); Jack Burns (1888); Hugh Kirkaldy (1891); Willie Auchterlonie (1893) and Sandy Herd (1902). Jamie Anderson died in penury at the Poor House, Thornton, Fife[38] in 1905, which is a sad end for anyone, but particularly bitter for someone who was a winner three times in succession. He was brought back to the Cathedral and buried in an unmarked grave. The graves of Tom Kidd and Bob Martin are also unmarked.[39] You would have thought that Anderson, Kidd and Martin, who won six Opens between them, merited at least a headstone, but apparently not. My last pick from the dead and buried would be Andra' Kirkaldy, who lost in the play-off for the 1889 Open. I would select him for his wonderful face (there is a magnificent portrait of him in the R&A) and for his wit. When playing with A.J. Balfour (Prime Minister, 1902-5) Kirkaldy took four to extricate himself from a bunker on the 17th, and in the process turned the surrounding air blue. When Balfour pointed out that he had been swearing, he replied, 'Swear! Not me. I said nae mair than a meenister would say in the pulpit if a fly settled on his nose.'[40]

CHAPTER 3

The Harbour

THE ORIGINAL PORT OF ENTRY to St Andrews was on the Eden estuary, at Guardbridge,* where the road to Dundee turns off the A91 to Edinburgh. It used to be known as the 'Water of Eden,'[41] which is a label that marketing men would kill for. St Andrews' natural harbour was first walled around 1100, and not before time. It quickly buzzed with activity. In 1337, over 30,000 pilgrims came to St Andrews,[42] many of them by ship, and that is a huge number of pilgrims and a huge number of ships.† Then there was the support industry: the merchants bringing in timber, iron, gunpowder, grain and flax from the northern ports in Scandinavia and the Baltic, and wine, nuts, spices and luxury clothing from the southern ports in the Netherlands and France. Everything required for a bustling city, stacked to the gunnels as it was with acquisitive and indulgent clerics, came in. No duties were levied on imports (only on exports!) and no holds were barred. In 1451 a camel was imported from Bruges for the Scottish Court[43] and, in 1474, a lion,[44] though how either survived the Scottish winter is not recorded. It was two-way traffic. The locals were not slow to come up with goods of their own to export: salted fish, wool, skins and fulmar feathers.[45] What anybody did with fulmar feathers I don't know (arrow flights perhaps), but if you want to see what a fulmar looks like there is a burgeoning colony by the castle cliffs. All this made for the sort of thronging and jostling harbour that would

---

* Guardbridge (lit: the station [gare] by the bridge) was also the site where pilgrims gathered before setting out on the final stage of their journey to the Pilgrim City. The original wooden bridge across the Eden blew down in a storm taking with it some 15-20 clerics, but its stone replacement, erected by Bishop Wardlaw in 1419, still stands. It runs parallel to the new road bridge and the stumps of the railway bridge on the Leuchars to St Andrews line. If you want to see it, you will have to get out of the car.

† Bear in mind that these ships were small. The age of the ocean liner had not yet arrived.

provide work for plenty of extras if anyone ever decided to make the movie: harassed cargo handlers supervising the loading and unloading of the continental vessels; merchants strutting around in their finery; customs officials poking their noses in where they were not wanted; gossip about piracy (of which there was plenty); coaster captains setting off for the less salubrious delights of Leith; and a salty old fisherman stepping ashore with a herring perched jauntily in his bunnet.

And then, during the 17th century, the referee called time and the game was over. The hustle and bustle was gone. Trade in and out of the harbour was down to a trickle. The old Church, with its expensive tastes and deep pockets, was no more. Continental wars had damaged trade with the Netherlands and France. The locals were suffering from low income and high taxes (what else is new?), to say nothing of death in the form of starvation from crop failures, plagues and penury. Then, to cap it all, the pier, which had deteriorated to such an extent that no ships of any size could go in or out of the harbour, finally collapsed in 1655. Rebuilding of a shorter replacement started thereafter, with stone removed from the Cathedral and Castle, but St Andrews was in such a parlous state by that time that it had to put out the begging bowl. An emissary was dispatched to Cupar, Perth, Dundee, Montrose and Aberdeen 'to humbly supplicate their concern and assistance'.[46] Quite a comedown.

Worse was to follow. The sea trade didn't come back and, a century later, even the fishermen had just about had their chips. In 1745, a sudden and violent squall erupted in St Andrews Bay and caught the local fleet unprepared. Boats were smashed. Lives were lost. The fishermen decided there and then to pack it in. They turned their backs to the sea, and gave up their work of centuries[47] – which is extraordinary, isn't it? You would have thought that seamen and storms went together like trouble and strife, and that fishermen could take whatever the weather chose to throw at them. Apparently not. The French would call it bizarre, but then the French call just about everything bizarre. They think it's bizarre that we don't sign up to the single currency and hand over power to a bunch of unelected eurocrats – but that's another matter. Anyway, fishing didn't return to St Andrews for 60 years, and then only because the Town Council in 1803 bribed a fleet from Shetland to relocate.[48] There was a brief revival. There was even an experiment with running a passenger service to Leith (the port of Edinburgh) – but it didn't last. The net fishing is now long gone. No more haddock. No more plaice. Today, there are a few boats left which lay lobster creels, but that's it. Many fishermen became caddies. It was the obvious career move. In what other profession is experience of being drenched by oceans of freezing water an advantage? Not, mind you, that this change of occupation brought the fishermen great wealth. One former skipper, when asked by an occasional patron whether his caddying was doing well, replied, 'No Sir, verra bad! I'm just thinkin' o' buyin' a lookin'-glass to watch mysel' starvin'.'[49]

Over the years, the fishermen and their families had colonised the Cathedral end of town around North Street and Castle Street. This area used to be known as 'Fishergate', which had a certain logic to it, but is now known as 'Ladyhead', which doesn't. Fishergate was a separate community. It had its own school, its own Mission Hall and its own underwhelming ratio of beds to people. The families overflowed out of their houses and onto the street, where the women (mainly) would mend nets, gut fish, bait lines and do whatever was necessary to keep body and soul together. It couldn't happen in North Street today – the traffic wardens would be on to them as soon as they sat down. There was also a cramped warren of a place down by the harbour, which rejoiced in the splendidly grandiose title of the Royal George, no less. Other overcrowded and dilapidated tenements in town had similarly inappropriate sobriquets – the Great Western, the Great Eastern, the Pembroke – which just goes to prove the general rule that the grander the name, the poorer the quality. If you ever find yourself forced to stay in a hotel called 'Majestique' or 'Royale', expect cockroaches. The Royal George was condemned as a slum in 1935 and rebuilt, no doubt with the best of intentions, in 1965.[50] Not the architect's finest moment. The Gulag-concrete style, whilst it has its place – in downtown Volgograd – would not be everybody's choice as an integral part of a medieval harbour.

But the harbour anyway is in more of a mess than it should be. Pride of place goes to a café that began life as a temporary building more years ago than anyone can remember, and is still with us – good chips though. There is a huge Victorian gasworks alongside the eastern wall of the Cathedral which has been out of operation since the 1960s and could be removed without anyone shedding a tear. Then there is the view along the East Sands and up the coast past Kinkell Braes, which would be wonderful except for the eyesore that is the caravan park. It is not that there is anything wrong with the caravans per se. Any one of them would be perfectly acceptable in isolation. It is just that there are a great number of them and they are visible for miles around. They are probably visible from Angus, for all I know. It wouldn't surprise me if they were visible from the moon. The answer is simple – a lick of green and brown paint, judiciously applied. In other words, camouflage. It's cheap, it's effective and it wouldn't be the end of the world if a plane, looking for somewhere to jettison its fuel tanks, failed to notice it. The caravaners would just have to be slightly careful when sitting outside enjoying a quiet cigarette.

The best thing about today's harbour is the pier, which stretches way out into the water, and the walk along it, over the old looted stones and the ghosts of dead bishops, to the end. If you time your trip for a Sunday, after morning chapel, you will see a straggly line of students, wearing the famous red gown of the university, amiably strolling along the pier, there and back. When, on a hot summer's morning, I first saw this surreal promenade heading off into the North Sea, I thought I had stumbled onto the set of a Buñuel film. When I saw it in winter, when the wind and the waves were howling over the pier, and it was cold enough to freeze a ghost, I was tempted to believe that the students here were made of sterner stuff than their effete contemporaries further south. Subsequent observation, in other contexts has, however, rather dispelled that particular illusion. The student walk commemorates the heroic deeds of John Honey, a student of the university and a man of great strength. On 5 January 1800, he swam out five times to the sloop, *Janet of Macduff*, wrecked in the

Bay, and each time returned with a rescued man. For this, he was awarded the Freedom of the City, which was the very least that St Andrews could do for him. On 5 January, in any year, it is an act of bravery merely to put a toe in the water. When he died fourteen years later, never having fully recovered from a blow in the chest from a spar from the ship, an immense crowd turned out for his funeral. Undeterred by the fact that John Honey was a student of philosophy, the University named the Computer Science building after him.

If you walk up the hill that overlooks the pier, keeping the Cathedral on your left, you will come across some venerable stones that mark the outline of an old church, the Church of St Mary on the Rock. This was the second home of the Culdee monks. Legend has it that their first home was built on a rock beyond the pier until, in the 6th century, it was submerged beneath the rising waters of the North Sea. The Culdees, part of the Irish monastic tradition, are mysterious, shrouded in the fog of history, and therefore romantic. They were contemplative ascetics, severe in their religious life, but not apparently averse to female company. In fact most of them were married men 'whose sons often succeeded them in their office'.[51] Sounds like a sensible arrangement to me. If you are going to spend your days in a cold stone cell, with instruments of flagellation and denial all around, what could be more restorative than a little woman to come home to in the evening?

Just beyond the Culdee ruins is one of many fine examples of 1990s local authority *naff*. Facing out to sea are two plastic cannons, courtesy of the Council. What drives these people? Did somebody on a committee of grown men and women really stand up and argue the merits of spending public money on fake cannons? At least if they are going to fake it, surely they could have produced a decent fake. Couldn't they make the cannons out of metal? The only reason I have so far suppressed the urge to pick them up and chuck them into the sea is that I'm a coward. I don't want to be arrested and banged up for the night. I don't want to imagine that look of sorrowful bewilderment on the faces of my friends from the local solicitors, Borgia, Borgia & Medici, as they attempt to secure my release. However, if you are a tourist, they will never catch up with you. Go on. Go for it. Do your bit for posterity.

CHAPTER 4

The Castle

FURTHER ALONG THE CLIFF, on a promontory jutting out into the North Sea, is what's left of St Andrews Castle – which is not much. It's hard, indeed impossible, to imagine from these hunched ruins that it was once one of the great buildings of Scotland. It was a castle in the way we all imagine castles: massive stone walls, a drawbridge, and cannon that guarded the approaches to this great Scottish City on the eastern seaboard. But on top of all this, it was Ambassador Class accommodation, where the Bishops and Archbishops of St Andrews hung their mitres, entertained royalty and demonstrated their exalted status for all the world to see. In fact, a palace – complete with state apartments, courtiers and casts of thousands.[52] The papal legate, Piccolomini,* came here in 1435 (probably to persuade the Scots to attack the English[53]) and described the castle as the 'citta nella citta', the city within a city. It was the most lavishly maintained residence in all of Scotland, the sometime seat of government, and the setting for battles, murder, siege, and skulduggery.

The problem with having a castle that doubled as a palace was maintenance. Inconsiderate people, with no feel for interior decorating, kept taking pot shots at it. The first castle, in place by 1200, took a pasting during the War of Independence (1296-1328) and spent the best part of 30 years as a ping-pong ball batted back and forth between England and Scotland. The English occupied it in 1296 and then, for good measure, burnt St Andrews two years later (after Edward I had defeated William Wallace at Falkirk).

---

* Piccolomini fathered a child whilst on his visit to Scotland, although this didn't prevent him from becoming Pope Pius II. He also found time to commit to paper some interesting comments on the Scotland of his day. 'The women', he said, were 'fair and comely, but licentious.' He would know, I suppose. 'There is nothing the Scotsman will listen to with greater pleasure', he observed, 'than abuse of the Englishman.' Nothing much has changed there then. 'Wolves, however, are unknown.' That's a relief.

The Scots won it back when Robert Bruce thrashed Edward II's huge army at Bannockburn in 1314. The English returned in the 1330s (the stucco! the carpets!) and it took Sir Andrew Moray, the Regent of Scotland and an ingenious stone-throwing siege engine called the 'Boustour', to reclaim it in 1337.[54] Andrew Moray may have been a decent sort of commander, but he must have been a world-class pessimist, the sort of fellow who takes his wellingtons with him when the sun shines, on the grounds that it's bound to be pouring soon. No sooner had he recaptured the castle, than he decided that, to prevent it falling again into English hands, he would level it. Which he did. Now, this might have been a reasonable strategy if the castle had been in northern England, or even in the Borders, but St Andrews is 50 miles north of Edinburgh, for heaven's sake. If you are not going to defend St Andrews, where are you going to defend? John o'Groats? The Arctic Circle?

It was left to a man of vision and confidence in the future, Walter Trail, Bishop of St Andrews (1385-1401), to rebuild the castle on appropriately splendid lines. Trail was a decent, upstanding sort of fellow but, with a name that rolls around the tongue like 'Walter Trail', I suppose that was inevitable. 'Good old Walter Trail.' 'Walter Trail, the People's friend.' It certainly appears that he did his best in a wicked world. Bower says of him that 'he curbed clerics from worldly affairs and commerce', which is fair enough 'and' (your scribe's eyebrow is now raised) 'he restrained priests with concubines from all brothel-keeping.'[55] Ho, hum. Anyway, Trail found time between sorting out the peccadilloes of his lieutenants to re-construct the castle as a lop-sided pentagon, with five towers on each corner. He put the Bishop's room and Chapel behind the main entrance (as you come in), with the magnificently palatial Great Hall on the east side. (This, through unpardonable neglect, was allowed to fall into the sea in 1801.) Guests and servants lived in the towers, or in ranges built along the inside of the walls, and surprisingly by today's preferences, the kitchen staff had the sea view facing north. It made it easier to chuck out the slops.

After 1472, the incumbents of the castle were Archbishops

rather than plain ordinary Bishops, and 50 years later it was Archbishop James Beaton (1521-39) who took it upon himself to strengthen the castle against attack. These were troubled times for Catholic priests. The Reformation was in full swing across Europe and James Beaton himself was to order the burning of Patrick Hamilton and Henry Forrest for heresy. As good a time as any to pay attention to your defences. Beaton believed that an attack was

---

The Price of Success

The Castle was home to all sorts of prisoners, from the local youth in the cooler for a week or two, all the way up to the heavyweights – and none was more top drawer than Patrick Graham, the first Archbishop of St Andrews.[56] For him, the dictum that applied, and on which he had ample time to reflect while rotting in his cell, was that nothing is so dangerous in life as success. Graham, the great-grandson of King Robert III and, by 1465, Bishop of St Andrews, conceived the not unreasonable idea that as the Bishop of 'the chief and mother city of the realm', he should be elevated to Archbishop. Not being the kind of man to let good ideas fester, he took himself to Rome and, by 1472, had managed to persuade the Pope that Scotland deserved an Archbishop – himself. Now you might imagine that, when the papal announcement known as 'the bull of erection' – a phrase that I must assume has gained a good deal in translation – reached St Andrews, there would be general rejoicing all round. 'Our own Archbishop, at last. How wonderful! How good for St Andrews!' Not a bit of it. The King and the nobles were incensed because Graham had omitted to let them in on his plans for promotion. The University and the Bishops were up in arms because he was claiming revenues for the Archbishopric that they thought were rightly theirs. To cap it all, he found that he couldn't pay the Pope the price of his advancement, so the Pope was after him too. This was just about a full house. In fact, when he arrived back home, there was hardly anybody who wasn't in hot pursuit. The poor fellow was arrested and, with a nice touch of irony, incarcerated in St Andrews Castle, his own prison. Charges, infinitely more imaginative than anything we might dream up these days, rained down upon Graham's benighted head. He was accused of everything from 'giving cause of offence', to 'irregularity' (I have speculated about this but appropriate meaning continues to elude), to 'believing that he was Pope'. If he was not mad beforehand, accusations like these could well have tipped him over the edge. Deemed insane, he was shunted from prison to prison before he breathed his last in Lochleven Castle in 1478. He was, as a friendly biographer put it, 'a man without a crime proved, inferior to none of his time in learning and in character' – but a little light on the ways of the world, perhaps.

The Castle, viewed from the west
as it might have been seen (clouds of glory excepted) in 1543.

likely to come from the town side and replaced Trail's rectangular towers to the south with two massive circular gun towers. Part of the western one survives today and the size of the gun holes will give you a good idea of how imposing they must have been. As it turned out, it was Beaton's successor and nephew, David Beaton, Archbishop of St Andrews (1539-46), Cardinal of the Church, Chancellor of Scotland, Bishop of Mirepoix in France, dabbler supreme in Scottish politics and father of ten, who was going to need defending.

Scotland was split, as so often. The Protestant element favoured alliance with Protestant England. They wanted Edward, the son and heir of Henry VIII, to marry the infant Mary Queen of Scots. The ascendant Catholic element, with Beaton to the fore, favoured the Auld Alliance with France. So Henry began his 'rough wooing' of Scotland. He sacked Edinburgh in 1544, and threatened to destroy St Andrews,* stick by stick, stone by stone, with no creature to be left alive.[57] This might have come straight out of Clint Eastwood's *Unforgiven*: 'Any sonofabitch takes a shot at me, I'm gonna kill him, I'll kill his wife, all his friends, burn his damn house down.' Not a moment in St Andrews to be seen as a 'tool of England' unless you happened to be their side of enemy lines, a lesson that the Protestant preacher, George Wishart, overlooked (unhappily for him). Beaton had him strangled in 1546 and then burnt outside the Castle gates, whilst the Cardinal looked on from his window above.† The town is fond of marking the precise spot where these historic bonfires took place, and sharp-eyed tourists will find the initials GW swimming in a sea of tarmac at the point where the Scores meets North Castle Street. Beaton spent

---

* St Andrews escaped.

† At least this is how the story was handed down, but by then it was the Protestants who were writing history. Even if true, there would have been nothing very unusual about Beaton's behaviour. In fact, it would have been postively genteel. At the massacre of Amboise in 1560, the upper classes were lucky enough to be beheaded and quartered, whilst the rest were either thrown alive in sacks into the river Loire or thrown off the castle battlements with a rope around their necks. This was regarded as suitable after-dinner entertainment for the royal party, watching from the balcony of the King's castle and including the young Mary Queen of Scots, then married to Francis II of France.

the next three months doing the sort of things Archbishops of St Andrews liked to do – sleeping with his mistress, running the country, hunting heretics, entertaining lavishly and worrying whether the carpets clashed with the curtains. Clerics, guests, soldiers and interior designers came and went daily through the main gates and, on 28 May, were joined by some fifteen 'masons', with murderous thoughts on their mind. They entered Beaton's chamber and knifed him to death. A pair of sheets were tied to his wrist and ankle, and his body was hung, naked and bleeding, from the walls of the South East Tower.[58]

As it happens, Cardinal Beaton lives on as Cardinal Smeaton in one of the best holiday golfing reads you are likely to come across – *The Haunted Major* by Robert Marshall, first published in 1902, and reprinted many times since. The Major, the Honourable John William Wentworth Gore, who has never hit a golf ball in his life, challenges the amateur champion of the day, Jim Lindsay, to a match at St Magnus for the right to propose to the beautiful and rich Mrs Gunter. Unable to sleep before the match, Gore finds himself heading along the Scores 'as the great trees bent and creaked in the wind' and 'the sea in a riot of black and white hurled itself with unabated fury against the adamant rocks'. Reaching the Castle at the witching hour and with the moon full out, he is grabbed by the ghost of the dead Cardinal. Smeaton is anxious to take revenge on Lindsay, the descendant of one of his murderers, and lends Gore his old set of magical clubs . . . The local bookshops should be able to provide a copy.

What happened after Beaton's death? The Protestants finding themselves in possession of the Castle, probably to their great surprise, decided that they might as well stay there – which, for the best part of a year, they did. The Catholics, led by the Regent, the Earl of Arran, wanted them out, of course – you can't just murder a Cardinal, occupy a castle and expect life to carry on as usual. Their first idea was to try to tunnel their way in. Not a bad plan, I suppose. At least it leaves the real estate intact. The only problem was that the defenders, no doubt hearing worrying tapping noises coming from down below, burrowed down to stop them.* The next move was brute force. The French navy was whistled up. It sailed into St Andrews Bay and bombarded the Castle from the sea, whilst the Catholics in town hauled heavy artillery up to the top of both St Rule's Tower and St Salvator's, and proceeded to pepper the Castle from there. Actually, not just the Castle. Cannon balls rained down on all and sundry and one such was found at 109 North Street while it was being rebuilt in 1932.[59] Entry was finally achieved, and the Protestants, including a certain John Knox, were rounded up. Knox was sent to the galleys and spent the next couple of years hauling an oar to the rhythm of the overseer's lash – a turn of events he had not predicted and which did little to make him a sweeter and more reasonable member of the human race.

The artillery bombardment of the Castle had left it in a right old state once again, and it fell to Beaton's successor, Archbishop John Hamilton, to effect repairs. The parts that you see from the street are largely his work, decorated by his five-pointed star, and for a fleeting moment, the Castle recaptured its former glories. But the phoenix was scarcely above the ashes when, in 1559, the Castle was back again in the hands of the Protestant reformers for whom pomp and the vestiges of its Catholic inheritance were anathema. Puritanisation took hold and neglect followed after. In the 1650s, the stones were being used to repair the harbour, and the slates and timber were sold off for ready cash. By the early 1800s, the courtyard, once the arena of kings and bishops, cooks and courtiers, tinkers and tailors, had been ploughed up for potatoes.[60] Creation is a struggle. It takes imagination. It takes energy. It takes years. Destruction is the breathless work of moments. St Andrews has had more than its share of both.

---

* The resulting mine and countermines are, apparently (if you are into this sort of thing), one of the most interesting pieces of siege engineering to survive anywhere in Europe. Even without specialist knowledge, they are well worth a grope and stumble down into the rock underpass to have a look.

When is a dungeon not a dungeon?

The Castle has a black hole, known as the Bottle Dungeon which is 30ft deep, 27ft across at the bottom, and 7ft across at the top. A bit like a vast claret decanter. When you come across something called the bottle dungeon, the natural assumption is that prisoners were incarcerated within. The official Castle Guide has pictures of prisoners languishing down below and quotes John Knox as saying that 'Many of God's children were imprisoned here'. There is an alternative theory, however (proposed by Jurek Pütter), that the 'dungeon' was carved out of the rock as a grain silo. Now the storage of grain was a problem in the Middle Ages because, if done badly, could lead to contamination by a fungus called ergot. This was an hallucinogenic, similar to LSD, which has been blamed for mass outbreaks of medieval hysteria, and for people trying to fly from the roofs of buildings. Ergot poisoning was supposed to have been the reason why Joan of Arc heard voices. The bottle dungeon is the perfect silo: it could hold over 180 tons of grain, was dry and had a stable temperature that varied by no more than three degrees a year. Jurek Pütter, by the way, is probably the only man for 350 years to spend two days and two nights down there (in 1966): it being the only place in Britain where he could be sure of not having to watch England win the World Cup. His ergot consumption is undisclosed.

Travels on the
Old Course

CHAPTER 5

The Opening Holes

Hole 1: Burn

MOST GOLF COURSES are situated decently far away from the prying eyes of passers-by, but at St Andrews you hit off from what feels like the middle of town, watched by a motley crew of townspeople, golfers, caddies, the ancients of the R&A, Uncle Tom Cobley, who have all seen the greatest golfers in the world drive off from this very spot – Jack Nicklaus, Tiger Woods and now you – and who are all only too eager to intrude upon what should be your own private grief. As knee-buckling experiences go, standing on the first tee of the Old Course is up there with the best of them. Prayer can be helpful. 'Please God, if I have ever done anything decent in my life, reward me this one time with something fairly near the middle of the club. At least, O Lord, spare me the airshot.' Eisenhower couldn't bear the thought of just that and walked to the second tee. For a General, and a man who once held the future of the free world in the palm of his hand, this was not the finest example of courage under fire. George Bush has recounted how when, in the early days of Czechoslovakian freedom from communism, he spoke in Wenceslas Square before one million people, his voice was clear, his knees were steady, and his pulse was regular. When he teed off at St Andrews for the first time, his palms were sweaty and his pulse had his attendants reaching for the beta-blockers. I know how he felt.

If nerves get the better of you, you may find you have sliced your drive over the white fence that runs alongside the right-hand side of the first fairway. In which case, give thanks to George Bruce, citizen and Town Councillor, that your ball is merely out of bounds and not in the sea. Before Bruce built the embankment that bears his name, water used to come up to the white fence and, at particularly high

'The Man who Missed the Ball on the First Tee at St Andrews.'

tides, wash over the course. The Victorians, not sharing our qualms about interfering with nature, moved the sea. Fair enough – that kind of thing certainly worked for Holland – but it can have a downside. The Dunes on the West Sands are being eroded because (and I rely here on local geologists who ought to know) the sand, which had been deposited, is now being diverted by the embankment elsewhere. When, one day, the sea breaks through the dunes and floods the Old Course, causing not only its demise but the subsequent demise of the local economy, we may regret Bruce's legacy but, until then, I am very pleased not to have to take out a new ball every time my controlled fade gets caught on the wind.

Snaking across the first fairway, in front of the green, is the Swilken Burn, the only hazard on an opening hole that is without rough or bunker and is wide enough to land a jumbo. In the old days, the burn was a proper hazard. It was wider, it was unkempt and it was covered in laundry. The women of the town had the ancient right to wash and bleach their clothes in the burn and lay them out on the fairway or surrounding whins* to dry. This caused

* Whins are gorse bushes. They have attractive yellow flowers. They attract golf balls.

a few problems, as you may imagine. There was the distraction for a start. It can't have been easy to play your second to the green, when the fairway was littered with shapely and vulnerable bodies, on all fours, scrubbing. Then there were questions about the rules. In 1851, the Rules Committee decided that when a ball was lying on clothes, or within one club's length of a washing tub, *the clothes or the tub could be removed*. Now, just picture the scene for a moment. A St Andrews housewife has been hard at her washing all morning and has her sheets nicely pegged out on the fairway, when a grubby old ball lands on them. Not far behind is a golfer who politely asks her whether she would prefer him to hit the ball where it lies – that is by standing on her sheets and ripping into them with his niblick – or whether she would like to remove the washing she has spent the last half-hour laying out. It may not come as a surprise to discover that, by 1888 – after thirty-seven years of golfers being berated by their mothers who had just met Mrs Henderson in the fish shop, and she had told her that she was washing her clothes by the burn when you came along and asked her to move them, and I've never been so ashamed in all my life – the rule was changed so that a ball lying on clothes could be lifted and dropped without penalty. And quite right too.

A fair few things have fallen into the burn over the years. Golf balls rain down on it daily, followed at lengthier intervals by golfers surveying a putt on the first green and taking one step backwards too many. Sometimes people have fallen in *en bloc*. In the 1920s, some stewards, who had obviously had too much porridge that morning, were using a rope to control spectators when they managed to sweep the entire multitude into the Swilken.[61] Probably did them a power of good, but it does make one curious about the subsequent exchanges between those same stewards and the members of the public who had been unceremoniously deposited in the drink. Did they opt for an opening gambit along the lines of: 'Here, Madam, let me give you a hand. No bones broken I hope'? Or did they down tools and leg it for the safety of the clubhouse before their victims could regain dry land? History does not relate.

There have been some high scores posted on the first hole

down the years, but the twenty-one strokes taken by Vicenzo Lunardi in 1785 might take some beating. Behrend and Lewis in their excellent *Champions and Challenges*,[62] relate how Lunardi, the first balloonist into English airspace, indeed the first person to penetrate said airspace if we exclude those who had overdosed on ergot, had set off on a similar voyage from Edinburgh on 5 October and an hour and a half later landed in a field between Ceres and Cupar.* 'The reapers stood stock still, petrified,' said Lunardi, 'imagining the moon was falling out of the sky and, when the man in the moon spoke to them through a silver trumpet, they fled in panic.' On the strength of his exploits, Lunardi was invited to play the Old and watched by a large crowd, took twenty-one shots going down the first. Probably a long round thereafter. The young Italian seems to have made quite a hit, because he was made an honorary member of the R&A, given the freedom of the town, and at the Provost's Ball was entertained by 'upwards of one hundred beautiful ladies'. Italians! They come here, frighten our farmers, seduce our women, play golf badly, and we still give them the keys to the city.[†]

Hole 2: Dyke

On your way to the second tee, glance across at the Himalayas[††] which, founded in 1867, is the oldest Ladies Golf Club in the world, probably. It was (and is) a putting club, which was put

---

* Ceres is a local village, Cupar a local town.

[†] There was another side to Lunardi. He was a member of a clandestine Scottish sex club, the Beggar's Benison: an affiliation he shared with George IV, several Earls, a bishop, and sundry merchants, landowners, customs officers and even smugglers. The Club was founded in 1732 and met annually in Anstruther, which is just down the coast from St Andrews. The entertainment included watching local girls dance naked, measuring penises on a special pewter plate and toasting the society with the words 'May your purse naer be toom (empty) and your horn aye in bloom'. The Club's artefacts are now in the capable, and discreet, hands of St Andrews University.

[††] There are not many flat putts on the Himalayas, as you may imagine.

there in order to prevent a simmering conflict[63] between the caddies and wives of R&A members from coming to the boil. Some time before 1860, the caddies had colonised an area (where Rusacks Hotel is now) for their own private putting circuit: somewhere to pass a few quiet hours and tighten up their technique. The Ladies, passing by, noticed this and thought 'how nice, a putting green' and started to use it themselves. The caddies resented the intrusion but were in a difficult position because the wives of R&A members often helped them out when times were hard, and anyway they wanted to carry on caddying for their husbands. So they didn't say much, although St Andrews caddies would not be St Andrews caddies if the odd pawky one-liner did not find its way into the ear of the appropriate husband. By whatever medium, the R&A got the message and organised the present site for their womenfolk. It is now open to the public (regardless of gender).

On the subject of over-starched Victorian ladies, you may wish to ponder this question, as posed and answered by Bobby Burnet, the R&A's historian (now retired), how ladies in days gone by, dressed in bodice and corset with wasp-waists, who could hardly do more than move five degrees from the vertical, were able to bend down and pick their ball out of the hole. With the Dey's patent ball-returning tin[64] that had been installed on every hole on the Himalayas in 1908 – that's how. You simply tapped the tin with your putter and the ball popped out (presumably, like toast out of an over-energetic toaster). Now, as inventions go, this may not be quite up there with penicillin and the jet engine, but for back sufferers and those afflicted by the ravages of time, it's not to be derided. That's not to say it is the complete solution. As one caddie commented at the time, 'It's no the getting' o' the ba' oot o' the hole that's the deeficulty, it's the getting' o' it in.'[65]

The old game was a running game, played with wooden clubs. With the price of golf balls what it was (we'll come to that), to attack a delicate hand-stitched featherie with an iron was a short cut to penury. The game was played low to the ground and a route had to be plotted around terrestrial impediments rather than over them. There was no reaching for the titanium, hitting the ball high into the air and watching it screw back on landing.* You don't get a feel for how much more difficult things were on the first hole, because it is immaculate and tonsured and staged, but you certainly do on the second. When you cast your eye over the rough that runs up the left, the whins on the right, the bunkers liberally sprinkled and the large egg-shaped lumps laid on the green by nature herself, you start to appreciate how good some of the old scores were. Allan Robertson's 79, shot in 1858, was a minor miracle – miraculous because he was playing with a gutta ball and wooden clubs of the sort you will see in the British Golf Museum, on a narrower and rougher golf course, with bunkers that were unraked and across greens that were better suited for grazing sheep than for putting. Minor miracle be hanged. It was a major miracle.

Hole 3: Cartgate (out)

There is an uninspiring piece of scrub land in front of the third tee, which grows over a mound and sundry assorted nasties beyond, which has to be driven. Provided you get the ball airborne, all should be well. I did hit a seagull once which was flying over this mound, but I don't recommend you follow suit. Apart from anything else, it took yards off my drive and years off the poor bird. Seagulls, as I now know, are tough. This one didn't die immediately, as any other animal hit by a Titleist doing 200 mph would have done, but lay on the ground miserably flapping its wings and looking at me accusingly. I should have walked up to it and dispatched it there and then as an act of mercy, but the fact was that I hesitated for one fatal moment, and didn't. Bear in mind that a seagull is a big oily bird, it reeks unpleasantly of fish, it has acquired a considerable inner strength on account of battling it out with the elements in extremely adverse conditions, and it has a sharp beak. That's what I saw when I looked over at the red cor-

* The first person to achieve backspin, by the way, seems to have been Jock Hutchison, a St Andrean turned American, who used it to win the 1921 Open. The R&A immediately declared his rib-faced mashie niblick illegal.

ner. In the blue corner was, well, me. To be frank, when it comes to wringing necks, I am inexperienced. I've usually left that kind of thing to my wife. I needed backup. Turning to my companions for assistance, I realised at once that any appeal I might frame would fall on ears that were not only deaf but, by this time, half way up the fairway. So I did what any golfer would do when the fourball behind is on the tee. I walked on. When I looked for the bird again on the 16th, it was gone, but I think of it from time to time, and that slight twinge I feel might be my conscience.

Talking of doing things to death, a farming friend of mine recounted how he was driving through Kennoway, a village in deepest Fife, when he had the misfortune to run over a cat. This was doubly unfortunate in that the event took place in front of a bus stop, where there was a queue of some five or six good local ladies of advancing years. Getting out of the car to investigate, he thought he should make absolutely sure that the cat was dead, so he picked it up by the hind legs and gave it a karate chop to the back of the neck. The matrons looked on appalled. Then, for good measure, he struck the unfortunate animal once more, dropped it in the road, and before his audience could recover its powers of speech, proceeded back to his car. Whereupon the cat got up and ran away.

The third hole has only one hazard of note and that is Cartgate: one of those bunkers not recommended for visitors who are losing ground on the fourball in front. If one of your party disappears, walk up to the edge and peer over. You will probably find him down there hacking away, shovelling buckets of sand onto the green and humming the first tune that comes to mind: something like 'Down among the dead men'. Best not to intrude. This is all part of the 'Old Course Experience'. There used to be, and we are talking here of the last century, another smaller bunker nearby called Tam's Coo which, according to legend, marked the spot where Old Tom Morris made his entry into this world. Tam, a farmer, had a milk cow which he used to tether on that spot. This cow was reported to have been so moved by witnessing the events that led to the birth of the great man, that it dug the bunker known subsequently as Tam's Coo.[66] Now you may wonder, as I

do, whether the concavity was brought about by birth or conception. I can quite see that witnessing a birth might, if the cow was of a sensitive disposition, have led it to dig a deep hole, except that recent research, and now a Council plaque, insists that Tom Morris first saw the light of day at 121 North Street (on 16 June 1821). Hence, the finger rather points at conception, although I have to say that most cows who regularly spent their nocturnal hours on the Links would, surely, have been inured to watching conception. And who was it that identified Mrs Morris anyway? It remains a mystery, but I can confirm that this coo's one enduring contribution to the life of man, endures no longer. The bunker has been filled in.

Hole 4: Ginger Beer

One of the things that the Old Course doesn't have, and that every golf course in North America does, is refreshment. It is just not possible to play eighteen holes in the United States without coming across a drinks buggy or a half-way house. It is taken for granted that an American golfer reaching the ninth hole may not have eaten since leaving the clubhouse two and a half hours earlier, and is therefore in urgent need of sustenance. Hence, golf courses lay on an instant menu that would do justice to a medium-sized Happy Eater. Very welcome it is too. Nothing like that exists on the Old Course today, although in years gone by we led the world in this kind of thing. Not for nothing is this hole called Ginger Beer. It was named in honour of the mobile refreshment cart pulled by David (auld Da) Anderson (1819-1901), which spent most of the year behind the 9th green but in the depths of winter was moved to the 4th, for the very good reason that the ideal time to catch your customers is just before they perish of hypothermia. By the 9th, they might be beyond reviving. Auld Da's cart was laden with ginger beer but, round the back, stronger beverages were available. The old prints of the drinks trolley don't provide any evidence of anything sizzling on a barbecue, but the idea of refreshment had clearly been established. It is (Links Trust please note) time for a comeback.

David Anderson was not just a pedlar of beverages. He enjoyed, if that is the right word, a life that swung violently between the best of times and the worst of times. His father, James, progressed from being a fraudulent bankrupt, to a man who minted his own sixpenny coins with which to buy ale,* to a convict transported to Australia.[67] He also found a spare moment to become a bigamist. Anderson senior was nothing if not creative. He decided to salt away a few small items in a secret closet in his mother's flat where he thought (mistakenly) that his creditors wouldn't find them – such as a mahogany chest of drawers, a four-poster bed and 38 gallons of whisky. 'Ma mither hae a saft side tae a wee dram, M'lud.' If so, not as much as he did. In his house, they discovered 150 gallons of the stuff. In spite of these distractions, David grew up to become a ballmaker (to Allan Robertson), a respected caddie and Keeper of the Green for the R&A. He had two sons, David who became a successful clubmaker, and Jamie, winner of the Open three times in succession from 1877 to 1879. This must have been a moment of enormous pride for auld Da, but thereafter things seem to have gone downhill. Twenty-six years later, and a mere four years after the death of his father,

* The charge brought before the courts was for 'uttering base coin'.

Jamie died in penury and, as mentioned earlier, was buried in an unmarked grave in the Cathedral grounds.

The interesting feature of the 4th hole is the 'latrines'. Imagine, running along the length of the hole, the arrangement common in most 'gents', except in green rather than porcelain. The sides of the 'urinal' extend into the landing area at the length of a respectable drive and catch anything a touch misdirected. This provides two routes from the tee: direct or safe. Direct is straight ahead with little room between the bunkers on the right and the latrines in the middle. Safe is out to the left, but it leaves a longer approach.

Hole 5: Hole o'Cross (Out)

The fifth is the first par five, and the stroke index of one would have you believe it is the most difficult hole on the course (which it isn't). Visible in the far distance is the left of a pair of bunkers called the 'spectacles'. Aim at the left spectacle. It is 430 yards away and famous for the fact that, in the 1933 Open, Craig Wood drove into it – which must have been painful for him since he went on to lose the Championship in a play-off. All the same, 430 yards was not a bad hit even by the standards of Tiger Woods. The longest recorded flight through the air with a gutta was in 1893 by Freddie Tait.[68] The ball flew 245 yards, and then bounced along the frozen ground to end up pin high on the 13th, 341 yards away.[69] As a result, Tait became famous overnight, but even his blow pales into insignificance behind one delivered to an old featherie in 1836 by Samuel Messieux. This was played on Hole o'Cross coming the other way and travelled 360 yards into Hell bunker.[70] Make what allowances you like for 'the slightly frosty day with a gentle following wind', this was still monumental. And yes, there were witnesses.

The fifth green is elevated and protected in front by a hollow, which is not visible from the fairway below. The main defence is, however, sheer size. This green is huge, the largest of the double greens in St Andrews and possibly the largest green in the world.

It measures over 6,000 square yards – big enough for a game of football. Hence, when considering what club to play for your approach, make sure you know where the flag is. Merely being on the green does not guarantee two putts. If you are so far away you can hardly see the flag, you may find yourself, as your grasp your putter, asking the question: 'Am I taking enough club?' Calcavecchia once hit a wedge on one of St Andrews' greens (not this one) and took a divot the size of a dinner plate, but I don't recommend you do likewise. It won't endear you to the green keepers. It didn't endear Calcavecchia.

Hole 6: Heathery (Out)

All you have to do on the sixth is to locate and then hit over a small and unobtrusive white marker post. Since no reachable part of the fairway is visible, there is no need to worry about what lies on the other side. Then hurry on after your ball, because the locals like to play round fast – meaning, in not much more than three hours, and certainly under four. Anything longer than this is a major cause of cardiac arrest. Unsurprisingly and understandably, visitors take a rather different tack. Pilgrims who make it to the Holy Land don't want to say a quick Hail Mary and then jump on the next camel home. They want to savour the moment, regard the monuments in deference and then stand lovingly on the hallowed turf before smashing plate-sized divots out of it. That's why we have 'rangers'.* To avoid bloodshed.

Golfers, of course, are endlessly inventive in the ways they find to hold up play. Some stand motionless over the ball for so long before hitting that it is possible to watch the rough grow up around them. Then there are the weight shifters, endlessly moving their weight from foot to foot. A local golfing farmer who did this said it was because he had farmed all his life on wet land. Andra Kirkaldy told one such: 'It's no' a pro ye need – it's a

---

* A ranger is an employee of the Links Trust who will gently coax those who are losing ground on the match in front into a higher gear.

dancing maister!'[71] Others feel that nothing less than five practice swings will do. Others like to pose for photographs. And so it goes. Nothing I have seen, however, quite compares to the member of an Egyptian club in the 1910s who, after a fairly decent stroke, was reported to drop his club and produce a pair of field glasses. He would then scan the immediate countryside (or perhaps, it being Egypt, desert) for a glimpse of his elusive spheroid and would only proceed after it when sure he had locked on to its co-ordinates.[72] Fortunately that practice did not catch on at St Andrews, or play would now take so long that field glasses would have to be fitted with infra-red night sights.

CHAPTER 6

The Loop

Hole 7: High (Out)

The Old Course has been described as Lesson 1 in knot tying. The course comes out from the town, loops around at the turn and crosses over itself on the way back. I seem to recall that Dale Robertson in Wells Fargo wore something similar round his neck, but I may be wrong. Anyway, the 7th, with a dogleg to the right, is where the knot starts. The ground in front of the tee is rough and unkempt in a natural kind of way, and spattered with whins like chocolate buttons on a birthday cake. Give yourself over to reverie for a moment, and you can just about imagine what the land must have been like when the game was starting out: when the Links provided sparse grazing for sheep, a playground for rabbits and just enough space between the whin bushes for golfers to put down some kind of rough hewn wooden ball and take a whack at it.

Animals, and not just rabbits and sheep, have always been a feature of the Old Course. A hundred years ago and more, Sir John Low and Mr Wolfe Murray, both R&A members, used to ride round on their ponies, and both took caddies, Wolfe Murray taking two: one to hold the horse and the other to hold the clubs. The caddies would fight for the easier job of holding the pony.[73] Wolfe Murray (while we are on the subject) was also an archer of repute and, on one noted occasion, challenged young Tom Morris to a match: bow and arrow against club and ball.[74] From tee to green, Wolfe Murray had the edge (particularly, no doubt, when it came to gingering up slower players in front), but he didn't find it easy to sink the final putt, so to speak. Not surprisingly, since the target was on the ground facing upwards, thus presenting no more than a slim crescent for the bowman to aim at. Wolfe Murray would have found it even more daunting if the holes had had tins in them, as now, but, in those days, holes were tin-less: the caddies using them as quarries, digging into them with their nails – sometimes up to their arms – to retrieve enough sand to make a tee. Clearly, however, our toxophilitic rough-rider managed to work out a method, because he won the match, having, in every sense of the word, shot the lower score.

The other beasts that roamed the course, and still do, were dogs. Man's best friend was there not only to sniff for golf balls, but also because there is something about a dog that improves a round of golf. I always take my retriever, and give thanks that St Andrews is one of the few places left where dogs are not *verboten*. She stands still when I hit. She doesn't talk at the top of my backswing and, when not admiring the wonderful way I strike the ball, is content to shuffle along unobtrusively in the rough. In fact, if I had to be reincarnated, I would want to come back as my dog. Her life consists of three activities. She eats, she sleeps and she plays golf. Unlike the other females in our family, she finds no reason to question the rationale, good sense and absolute authority of her master, and thus enjoys a life of abundant pleasure, at peace with her surrounds. If she has one small fault, it is her passion for wishing to disguise her scent with the canine equivalent of Chanel No.5. You may take it from me that there is nothing quite like the smell of a wet retriever that has rolled herself over and over on a rotting rabbit.

Hole 8: Short

The ancients who named the holes on this golf course were having a bad time of it when they reached the 8th. There they were, scratching their heads, puffing on their pipes, slowly opening their mouths as something inspired seemed to be clawing its way up from down below, and slowly closing them again. So the day passed. Mouths opened. Mouths closed. Heads were scratched. Pipes were puffed. Finally, up spoke Anon. 'Ye ken hoo th' echt hole is nay mair as 150 yairds. Hoo aboot we ca' it Short?' You may well imagine the rapturous acclaim with which this was greeted. And so pleased were they that, when it came to naming the one visible bunker, it was unanimously agreed to call it 'the Short Hole Bunker'. The names have stuck – and that's just about it for the 8th, except to warn you that the eponymous bunker which guards the green can be vicious. If your ball lands close to the face, forget it. Unless you can hit the ball up on a 6 to 1 gradient (6 feet vertically and 1 foot horizontally), either play out backwards or take a drop. Just make sure the bunker is a one stroke penalty, and not the beginning of something truly disastrous.

Hole 9: End

The 9th is dull. It is short, flat and boring. Even the name, 'End', produces a yawn. One of the first schools I attended had a Latin motto which was sewn onto our blazer pockets. *Lauda finem*, it read, 'Praise the end'. We all took this to mean 'praise the end of lessons'. To this day I am still not sure what it was supposed to mean. 'In the end we are all dead, so let's rejoice'? Possible, I suppose, but I can't imagine even my old school inviting us to praise the Grim Reaper and all his works. 'Praise the end (as opposed to the means)', perhaps? Well, we do hear that 'the end justifies the means', but if we taught that in British schools there is no telling what mayhem would ensue. 'I thought the world would be a better place without Smith, Sir, so I did him in.' There must be generations of schoolboys like myself who have gone through life saying to themselves, 'Hmn, lauda finem. I only wish I knew what that meant.' Perhaps that's the devilishly subtle point. Who knows. Anyway, I find myself unable to praise this particular 'End' beyond saying that it has one or two interesting bunkers. There are a couple on the shortish left from the tee, put in by Tom Morris during the Boer War and named Kruger and Mrs Kruger, after the Boer President (and his wife). However, the only ones that need concern you are the two down the middle, which stare you in the face off the tee and are a good deal easier to get into than out of. Actually, come to think of it, there is another bunker, just on the left of the green, that you can go for years without noticing, and that pops up when you really cream a drive. This is called Cronje, after the Boer leader who surrendered in 1900 following the relief of Kimberley. Fortunately, no sand traps were laid down during the Second World War or we might find our ball in the Adolf and Eva bunker.

Since the 9th is the Boer War hole, I should perhaps mention the best known golfing casualty of that war, Freddie Tait. Bernard Darwin, the doyen of golf writers, had this to say about him: 'In his day and in his own Scotland, he was a natural hero. I do not think I have ever seen any other golfer so adored by the crowd – no, not Harry Vardon or Bobby Jones in their primes.' Tait was a top class amateur in the Age of the Amateur* – but his record was certainly not superior to his great rivals, John Ball and H.H. Hilton.† His fame rests on other attributes, principally the priceless gift of being able to smile simply and unaffectedly on the world. The world was charmed into smiling back. He was devoted to family and friends, easy going, a by-word in courtesy to opponents, and definitely the sort of man who saw the means as infinitely more important than the ends. 'Tait was a very fine man,' wrote Herbert Warren Wind, 'whose only shortcoming was a tendency to play his bagpipes in the street late at night and wake up the whole neighbourhood.'[75] On 11 December 1899, he was leading his company in an attempt to force the Boers from their position at Magersfontein, when he was shot in the thighbone. He recovered well enough, only to be shot by a sniper's bullet two months later on 4 February 1900 on a reconnaissance operation at Koodoosberg Drift. He was 30 years old. His epitaph, taken from Wordsworth, reads, 'The good die first, And they whose hearts are dry as summer dust, Burn to the socket.'

---

* The amateurs were able to take on, and frequently beat the professionals, from roughly 1885 to 1930, the year that Bobby Jones retired.

† Tait's record includes winning the British Amateur twice (1896 and 1898) and, in 1894, lowering the course record at St Andrews (and Carnoustie) to 72 shots.

Hole 10: Bobby Jones

The 10th was probably a good hole in days gone by, but it has been undermined by titanium. The pros these days spot that it is 318 yards and ease back on the driver. Daly probably goes with the 3 iron. Mind you, it has been driveable by the long hitters throughout the age of steel and persimmon. Sam Snead drove the green three times out of four in the 1946 Open, which he won. The '46 Open was the first one after the War when Britain was still held tight in the anorexic grip of rationing. It can't be easy to put on a Championship when there is a shortage of paper for entry forms, and when one former champion, Arnaud Massy, writes to say that he will only be able to make the trip if the Board of Trade can find him some clothing coupons. Quite right. Former winners teeing off starkers – the mind boggles! Everything was tight. Dunlop wrote to the Secretary of the R&A saying that it would supply Dunlop '65' balls but that the amateurs were only allowed two each for the first and second qualifying rounds. (That would have been my chance blown right there.) As for food, the R&A was rooting around to provide something more substantial than the twelve Swiss rolls they had been able to cajole from the town bakeries. 'Pies', they reported, 'were out of the question on account of the restricted supplies of fat and meat.'[76] None of this bothered Snead. He probably didn't like Scotch pies anyway, and certainly wouldn't have if he had known what was in them. Snead flew in on Friday morning, practised, played through the qualifying rounds and, a week later, victory was his. When he was called on to come up and receive the trophy, he was still wallowing in his bath.[77] However, he bravely clambered out and held the claret jug aloft to warm applause. I only hope he had managed to scrape together enough clothing coupons for a bath towel.

You will probably have spotted that the 10th is called Bobby Jones after the legendary American golfer who won the Open here in 1927 (by a street) and the Amateur in 1930, the year of his Grand Slam.* Only one other person has had a hole on the Old

---

* The Grand Slam in those days was the Open and Amateur of Britain and the USA.

Course named after him and that was Tom Morris himself, so Jones was in good company. The town also gave Bobby Jones the Freedom of the City in 1958, and this hadn't happened to an American since they got the keys out for Benjamin Franklin all those years ago. You could say that he was a popular fellow around these parts. Mind you, if you asked local golfers what the

---

Scots bring golf to America

It was Scots like James Wilson (who signed the Declaration of Independence, and was probably a decent golfer given that he was educated in St Andrews), who first brought the game to America – and somewhat earlier than is normally supposed. Scottish merchants living in South Carolina imported clubs and balls into Charleston, in 1743.* During the American War of Independence, captured R&A members, like the Earl of Balcarries,† whiled away their confinement by working on their game[78] and, one might surmise, by passing on a few tips to their captors. 'Here, pass me that that rifle and let me see your backswing.' Scottish merchants formed the South Carolina Golf Club in 1786[79], and the Golf Club in Savannah around 1796. Incomprehensibly, given the present national love affair with golf, American golf clubs disappeared in the early 19th century and it wasn't until the end of that century that the first permanent golf club was founded in Yonkers, New York – by a Scotsman. Could one country do more for another?

---

* The Charleston *News and Courier*, 16 August 1978, has a reference to the ship *Magdalene Castle* sailing from Leith to Charleston in 1743 ' carrying eight dozen golf clubs and three gross of golf balls.'

† Balcarries, a.k.a. Alexander Lindsay, the above-mentioned POW, merits a word or two because he demonstrates both the possibilities for intercontinental travel in the 18th century, and the attractions of a charmed and cavalier lifestyle. He was Captain of the R&A at the age of 23 by virtue of winning the club championship in 1775. Two years later, according to Behrend and Lewis in their excellent history of the R&A, he found himself in North America commanding a battalion of light infantry under General John Burgoyne. At the battle of Ticonderoga in July, whilst storming the heights of Huberton, 13 musket balls passed through his jacket, waistcoat and breeches. Normally, this sort of thing would bring the curtain down on a promising career but, somehow or other, he contrived to exit the battle with only slight injuries. (Testimony perhaps to the armour-like properties of 18th-century woollen garments: a subject which is discussed further below.) Burgoyne then surrendered at Saratoga six days later and Balcarries became a prisoner of war. But at least he had his life, and plenty of time to practise his short game. He subsequently went to Jamaica, quelled a rebellion and became Governor. Still not entirely fulfilled, it is reputed that he fought a duel with Benedict Arnold, the American traitor. Arnold fired first, but missed, and Balcarries, rather than returning fire, responded with the majestic words 'Sir, I leave you to the executioner.' The only problem with this story is that Arnold lived to the age of sixty, unexecuted.

10th hole was called, I am not sure how many would know. The only name that everybody remembers is the Road Hole, the 17th, probably because the road is a hazard that they have found themselves on often enough not to forget. Golfers go round a course by number because names are disorientating and numbers are orientating. When you lie in your bath reliving the day's round, you don't say 'What a great drive I hit on End', you say 'I drove the 9th'. As to which hole follows another, I would be willing to bet that there aren't more than two golfers in St Andrews who know that Heathery (In) comes after High (In) and, if there are, they should seriously consider turning themselves in to the Memorial Hospital for a brain scan.

Hole 11: High (In)

Holes 8, 9 and 10 have some provenance going for them, but not a lot else. The 11th, however, which crosses over the 7th to make the knot in the tie, is a different kettle of fish altogether. It is about 170 yards from the back tees, with a green that not only slopes vertiginously from back to front, but is protected by two truly cavernous bunkers, Hill and Strath. The pin is frequently tucked behind Strath, offering extreme temptation to those of us who remain golfing adolescents and can't resist a challenge. This is a hole that used to bother the pros, with Bobby Jones famously having trouble here in 1921, but the difference nowadays is that instead of taking 5 and 6 irons they take 8s and 9s – which is positively unsporting. This is not to say that the old girl can't still jump up and bite the very best. Freddie Couples at the 1990 Open hit into Strath and, after two more, his ball was still below ground. 'This is it', we all thought, 'Goodnight, Fred', assuming that he would do as we would do, namely disintegrate into a quivering jelly. He didn't. He swung again in his usual relaxed manner, and the ball described a soft, gentle parabola before landing in the hole. Makes you sick.

Strath bunker is named in honour of three famous golfing brothers of St Andrews, Andrew, David and George Strath.

(Actually there was a fourth brother, William, who was frequently up in front of the sheriff court in Cupar for breaking and entering with assault,[80] but we may safely assume that he was not uppermost in the minds of the worthies who sat on the 'bunker committee'.) Andrew won the Open in 1865 and died three years later of tuberculosis at the age of 33. Davie, who was generally thought to be a better golfer than Andrew and on a par with young Tom Morris, had his chance in 1876, when he tied with Bob Martin in the Open at St Andrews.* However there had been an incident on the 17th green when Davie's ball, as reported by the *St Andrews Citizen*, 'struck Mr Hutton, upholsterer, who was playing out, on the forehead and he fell to the ground. We are happy to say that, though Mr Hutton was stunned, he was able to walk home'.[81] Whilst Mr Hutton was staggering back to his place of abode, no doubt to moan to his wife about how appalling it was that golfers playing in the Open should be allowed to interfere with his regular fourball, an objection was raised with the R&A that Hutton had 'checked the forward career' of Davie's ball and may have stopped it rolling onto the road. The matter was left with the R&A but, for one reason or another, they had not ruled on the matter prior to the play-off, and Davie was not prepared to play without a ruling. Probably not a good decision because Bob Martin walked over the course for victory, and two years later Davie was dying of tuberculosis. Rather than send him to the chemist round the corner, or for a couple of weeks in Spain, someone advised him that Australia would be good for his health. Australia! It's only half way round the world and 13,000 miles of heaving ocean away. By the time the ship arrived at Melbourne, Davie was dead. He was 29. TB was the great killer. It did for Andrew, his mother, his wife and his daughter, for William (probably) and Davie (certainly). They all died young. Young Tom Morris had died of causes unknown aged 24. His wife had died in childbirth. And so it went.

---

* Whilst Davie was playing his heart out, William was recuperating from a conviction in March for theft before the Police Court at St Andrews, and was planning his next heist – a break-in in Pilmuir Place – for which he was to get six months. Tom Morris was a witness but whether for or against is not clear.

All I can say is, thank heavens for the NHS. The only Strath brother not to be carried off early was George. He couldn't compare to Andrew and Davie as a golfer, but he was good enough to become one of a band of professional Scots golfers who helped to establish the game in the USA. He took up residence in Brooklyn and, since the threat of dying of TB there was negligible compared to all the other things in New York that might finish him off, he survived to the ripe old age of 59 – which for a Strath was positively geriatric.

Hole 12: Heathery (In)

Whatever you do, don't hit your drive down the middle. Hook it, slice it, bounce it off a passing seagull, but don't hit it straight. If you can carry the ball 240 yards, OK, I take it back, you can hit it straight, but otherwise don't. Hidden bunkers lurk. You may say this is unfair, secreting bunkers in places where golfers can't see them and right in the middle of the fairway to boot, but it all happened naturally and nature is, of course, blameless. The evolutionary process went something like this. Originally, or at least from the time that order began to be established, the Old Course was eleven holes out and the same eleven holes played back. In 1764, the R&A (or what was to become the R&A) took what looks like a unilateral decision[82] that the first four shortish holes should be converted into two longer ones. The Old Course was now played as nine holes out and back, thus giving the world eighteen holes of golf, rather than twenty-two: something for which wives who prefer their husbands at home rather than on the links should be properly grateful. In the early days, the course was laid out over what we now regard as the back nine (the left hand nine). By the early 1800s, the bright idea of putting two holes in each green[83] so that outward and homeward players could have their own flag, had begun to catch on. Then as the course was widened in the latter half of the 19th century, players enjoyed the luxury of separate fairways. The course could be played either by the left hand route (from the first to what is now the 17th, then to the 16th and so on) or by the right hand as used today. Twenty

years ago, the left-hand course was still played for a couple of weeks in winter, and this was exciting, like stepping through a chronological curtain and finding yourself back a hundred years. All those bunkers which you had been muttering about for years suddenly no longer seemed so unfair after all. Those that had seemed completely pointless and out of reach, even for some of the people I play golf with, suddenly acquired a purpose. Now no longer, alas. Our two weeks have gone. The gateway to the past has been boarded up by some kill-joy committee with a large red pen and no imagination.

As you leave the 12th tee, take care. There is ahead of you one of those bunkers that has no purpose at all when the right-hand course is in play – unless you really connect with a big draw from the 7th tee – but it can trap the unwary. It is known as the Admiral's bunker, after Admiral Benson who was distracted by the sighting of an attractive young lady wearing a red mackintosh. Uttering the immortal words, 'I wouldn't mind posting a letter in her box,'* he fell overboard and disappeared from view into the beckoning sand below. Benson is also remembered for going round the Old Course in a gross 88 strokes.[84] The year was 1965. It was on one of those days that St Andrews reserves for its

---

* Or something along these lines.

medals: when a frozen Force 10 howls out of the Arctic; when you have to walk down the first backwards if you wish to continue with basic bodily functions, like breathing; and when, should you make the mistake of touching your ear, it falls off. Benson was eighty-one years old at the time and of an age when resistance to exposure is not at its peak. Besides which, he carried a paltry six clubs, in a bag manufactured in 1893: which just goes to show.

CHAPTER 7

The Closing Holes

Hole 13: Hole O'Cross (In)

Beware. The closing holes can bite, and the 13th, which is a wonderful stretch of unspoiled links land, has teeth as sharp as any. It is defined by a rough meandering shelf that divides the hole into two segments, and a narrow gully, strewn with hidden pot bunkers, that cuts through it. The epicentre of the trouble, however, is the 'coffins' that catch the drive. When you come across bunkers called coffins, it is a mistake to assume that the ancients are being playful. I should warn you that it is not only golf balls, and your hopes and dreams, which can be interred. If you hang around too long, you risk ending up there yourself. This particular part of the golf course is the most dangerous piece of golfing country in the world,* and probably the most dangerous patch of ground, golfing or otherwise, between the North Pole and the Balkans. They can't see you from the 6th tee and you can't see them, and as you are contemplating your second, they are at the top of their backswing about to blast off straight at you. There have been casualties, of course. Brave men who have spat out their broken teeth, graciously accepted the apologies of their unwitting assailants – if they're Americans they will be petrified of being sued for every last cent – shrugged their shoulders, and played on. Brave men such as these do not allow images of their dentist, scrambling through the rubble of expensive bridgework, to break their concentration.

The Old Course has always been dangerous. When it was played out and back over 11 holes to the same green and the same

---

* With the possible exception of that stretch 150 yards short of the 12th green on the New Course.

hole, there must have been balls flying about all over the place. Rule 1 of the 1754 rulebook read '*You must Tee your Ball within a Club length of the Hole.*' Now this does paint a picture. For a start, the greens were obviously so rough that no one bothered about teeing off on them. One more scuff mark or one more divot was clearly neither here nor there. But what about the risk of being hit? There you are driving off on the outward nine, when the players on the inward nine are hitting towards the precise square yard of ground on which you are standing. I wouldn't have fancied it, particularly if I couldn't see them coming. It may not sound too painful being hit by a 'featherie' but, believe me, by the time the feathers had been soaked and packed down into a leather casing, those balls could inflict some punishment. You certainly wouldn't want to leap up and head one into an empty net. Perhaps that's why the ancients covered themselves with enough padding to keep out an elephant gun: stiff jacket, waistcoat, sturdy boots, and thick trousers. Judging by the old pictures, the trousers looked as if they were solid enough to stand up by themselves. Golfers in days gone by didn't need tee shirts and light gore-tex wind cheaters. They needed armour.*

Hole 14: Long

As anyone who has golfed will tell you, you can be playing along, the sun is shining, all is going tickety boo, when out of a clear blue sky, disaster strikes. If you have reached the 14th with your score intact, but start to feel a tingle in the back of the neck, take care. The 14th is as likely a place as any for the Fates to reach down and grab you. Anything is possible on this hole. I have known a five handicap golfer play his sixth shot from behind the tee – which takes a bit of doing – but even the truly great have problems. In the 1939 Open, Bobby Locke was six under fours standing on the tee, took two to get out of the nasty cluster of bunkers on the left

---

* Incidentally, one of the enquiries submitted to the R&A asked what the ruling would be on an incident when a player on his downswing missed his own ball but hit another ball coming in the opposite direction towards him. This actually happened.

called the Beardies, put his fourth in Hell and ended up with an eight. Next day, in order to avoid the beardies, he drove out of bounds over the old stone wall on the right and took seven. All this 'amazed South Africans back home because in four years of championship golf, he had never been known to take as much as a six.'[85] The place to put your drive is on the sunlit uplands known as the Elysian Fields, beyond which lurks Hell, a vast area of sand in the misleading shape of a malformed heart, with a vertical face ten feet deep. This is best avoided unless you have time on your hands. The Bishop of London is reported to have been so pleased to have got out at the first attempt that he felt moved to verbalise the experience. 'Out of Hell in one!' he exclaimed. To which Andra Kirkaldy, his playing partner, retorted, 'When ye dee, mind and tak' yer niblick wi' ye'.[86]

Hole 15: Cartgate (In)

If you fade your drive on the 15th, and land short of the mound on the right, you may find yourself on a pair of strangely evocative, rounded protuberances, known as Miss Granger's bosoms. If your ball comes to rest on one of them, or in the cleavage, you probably won't make the green with your second. It isn't easy to gaze down at your ball so cosily ensconced and envisage taking a divot. Innate reverence, or respect for the mysteries of life, prevents most of us from doing more than catching the ball thin and skinning it. I have no idea who Miss Granger was, but I have a picture of a young and comely Scots lass with a welcoming smile and with breasts – well, you have to see those for yourself. If it turns out she was an old bag, with scraggly hair and black teeth, I do not wish to know. There is one curious thing about her bosoms, though, and that is how elusive they are. You can be playing along and think, 'mmn, I'll just wander over and have a look at Miss G's bosies', but you won't find them. By some curious trick of the light, or modesty of nature, they are only visible to those who land on them. Her favours are not bestowed on the passing voyeur, which makes me think that my instincts about her are right. She was a good girl at heart.

If you wish to place yourself beyond temptation, hit it well left. Slightly left and you flirt with a little pot bunker called Sutherland which, after the charms of Miss Granger, is a much less enticing prospect. This bunker rocketed to prominence in 1869, when Tom Morris, as Custodian of the Links, decided to fill it in, only to find himself and the R&A Green Committee threatened by a lawsuit from one A.G. Sutherland. Sutherland was a solicitor, although since he spent his winters on the links at

Musselburgh and his summers at St Andrews, his active soliciting may have been on the wane. Anyway his view boiled down to 'What nature has ordained must not be tampered with by some jumped up Green Committee', which is a fair enough sort of sentiment. The battle raged until one night, under cover of darkness, a couple of R&A members reinforced by the local snake oil, sneaked down to the links bearing a wheelbarrow, spade and a local gardener, and restored the bunker to its former glory.[87] They left behind a notice bearing the legend, SUTHERLAND, and neither Tom Morris nor the Greens Committee were brave enough after that to bother it again.

Hole 16: Corner o' the Dyke

The 16th is a hole which proves that nature is a designer in a class of her own. From the tee, you can reach out and touch the out-of-bounds on the right. Don't flirt with me, it whispers, but there waiting for you on the left side of this narrow fairway is the Principal's Nose, with two nostrils hidden behind, and thirty yards further on, a treacherous little pot called Deacon Syme. The pros hit it miles left, which is boring. It hasn't always been out of bounds on the right. The old railway line, which came to St Andrews in 1852 and ran down the side of the 16th, used to be, by some curious ruling, in play. The main danger was not from the trains, which would be chugging gently to a halt at the sheds in front of the 17th tee, but from the fact that there are not many good lies to be had on a railway line. James Braid, who at the time was leading in the last round of the 1905 Open, described his experiences in the following disgruntled language: 'I got it onto the railway and . . . found it lying in a horrible place, tucked up against one of the iron chairs in which the rails rest . . . I took my niblick and tried to hook it out but did not succeed, the ball moving only a few yards, and being in much the same position against the rail. With my fourth I got it back onto the course but . . .'[88] He still went on to win.

Hole 17: Road

The 17th is quite simply one of the great holes in world golf. The line is over the dark green sheds in front of the tee, which are intended to replicate the old railway buildings. They have to be driven and, if you find the right line, the carry is 180 yards. Of course, the further right you go, the longer is the carry and you should bear in mind that the Old Course Hotel, which sprawls inelegantly beyond the sheds, does not return balls that land in its lap.* You may decide, somewhat wimpishly, that you would rather play left of the sheds, in which case you will land in the rough that divides the 17th from the 2nd. Your second shot will then be caught by the long grass and end up in Scholars bunker. From there, you will hack out to the appropriately named Progressing bunker, thence to the Road Hole bunker, from that bunker to the road itself, and from the road to a muted plea to your caddie to take you round the back and shoot you. Better by

* There is no danger to life for diners and residents, sheltered by the hotel's ball-proof glass, but they should take care when sitting out on their bedroom balcony with drink in hand. The balconies are in range from the tee.

far to take on the sheds and, if you perish in the attempt, at least the failure will have been noble.

The stand behind the green is the place to park yourself during an Open if, like me, you enjoy nothing better than watching great golfers come to grief. The green is a narrow, two-tiered undulating strip, protected at the front by the magnetic Road Hole bunker, now known locally as the 'Sands of Nakajima', after the eponymous golfer who self-destructed within. Well worth the entrance money, that was. Behind the green is the road, whose salient feature is that it is three feet or so beneath the hole, with a stone wall beyond. Not even Calcavecchia chips well off tarmac, so when a ball trickles off the top level of the green down on to the road, the only sound is the clack clack of knitting needles as Madame Guillotine and her crones, aroused by the smell of blood, lean forward in their seats.

Hole 18: Tom Morris

Grip your driver, suppress the thought that everyone leaning on the rails that run up the right side of the fairway must be mad – don't they know about my slice? – and let rip. I have often wondered who parks their car in Links Road, which is the lane that runs up the right. It certainly isn't the locals, who have a pretty good idea about what's what when it comes to protecting their worldly goods. They must all be hire cars. Golf balls smack into them regularly and, given a decent bounce off something substantial like a Volvo, stand a good chance of coming back into play. Sometimes the cars are missed and the houses beyond are hit. Sometimes, even these are avoided. One of the more charismatic golfers of my acquaintance sliced his ball to the right of the row of houses, down Gibson Place. While it headed erratically towards the A91 and into a stream of oncoming traffic, did we drop our clubs and rush to ascertain the extent of the vehicular mayhem, to see if we could pull any bodies from the pile-up, perhaps offer our gore-tex waterproofs until the ambulances arrived? Did we heck. This is St Andrews where the small matter of life and death cannot be allowed to hold up play.

The professionals normally save their dramatics for the green. Remember Constantino Rocca, with two shots from the valley of sin to tie with John Daly, fluffing the first and holing the next from 60 feet? Remember Doug Sanders in 1970, missing a downhill, left to right, three footer to win the Open? Nothing, though, compares to Leo Diegel in 1933 who needed two putts on the last to tie with Shute and Wood. He laid the first one stone dead and then had an air shot. With a putter! Gone was immortality. Gone was the *pied-à-terre* in St Tropez. One may only surmise what his wife said to him when he slunk home that night. I wonder if she remembered the immortal words of Bernard Darwin that 'a man may miss a short putt and yet be a good husband, a good father and an honest Christian gentleman'. Probably not. No grappling with the issue of personal worth for you, however. Two authoritative putts, a glance at your loved one leaning over the white rails behind the green, and hand shakes all round. Time then, over a quiet glass, to play through the round again, and reflect on what was, and on what might have been.

Further Travels
Around the Town

1425
A·D

CHAPTER 8

The University: early days

IF YOU WERE a Scot in the 14th century, were thinking about a university education, and were not put off by the thought that Scotland v England hostilities might resume at any moment, you would go to Oxford or Cambridge. Alternatively, if you didn't fancy England, there was always the Continent: Italy, Germany, the Low Countries or, most popular of all, France. On the basis that my enemy's enemy is my friend, France was a close ally, and there were enough Scots at the universities of Paris, Orleans and Montpellier to mix a little sandy colouring into the Gallic gene pool. By the 15th century, Scotland felt that it could do with its own university. Paris is a long way away if you want to bring some washing home at the weekend.

In 1410, a group of Scottish ecclesiastics, most of whom had graduated in Paris, gathered in St Andrews and formed a centre of higher education. This was the beginning of the University – except that it could not award degrees, and was not recognised as having university status. For this it needed the agreement of the Holy Roman Emperor or the Pope. Now, at the time, there were two popes, one in Rome and another, the Antipope Benedict XIII in Peniscola, Spain. As it happened, Scotland rather preferred the papal antidote, and so applied to Benedict who, no doubt flattered by the attention, was pleased to issue the appropriate papal bulls declaring St Andrews a university. These arrived back in town in 1414 and, amid great local fanfare, St Andrews took its place amongst the venerable universities of Europe.

The new University began life without any buildings of its own, which was not as odd in those days as it sounds now. A society of scholars can meet anywhere (provided it has friends with a spare room or two) and, in the first flush, not having to worry about a leaking roof or giving employment to an army of accountants, must have felt wonderful. Alas, as any married couple will tell you, such utopian freedom rarely survives, and it wasn't long before the University was on the property trail. The early home of the University appears to have been in South Street, but the first college to be founded was St Salvator's, in North Street, in 1450. St Leonard's, sited just off the Pends, followed in 1512 and St Mary's on South Street in 1537.

Viewed from North Street, St Salvator's Chapel and Tower look much the same today as they did in the 15th century, give or take a few statues that attracted Protestant displeasure, and were destroyed at the Reformation. Intertwined in the cobblestones, before the main entrance to the College, are the initials PH, commemorating Patrick Hamilton, the Protestant martyr, who was burned on this spot in 1528. Tradition has it that any student who stands on these fails his final exams, so if you see young men and women zigzagging around it, that's why. It is also said that, after PH had dissolved in flames, an etching of his face appeared spontaneously – that is to say without benefit of human intervention – in the stones of the tower above. There is no doubting there is a face there, somewhat impressionistic perhaps, but a face nonetheless, and when you locate it, you will be pleasantly amused at having done so. The arms of the College founder, Bishop Kennedy, are above the main gate, whilst at the top of the Tower hangs Katharine or Kate (Kennedy), the original college bell, accompanied by Elizabeth, the old bell from St Leonard's. The two old maids have rather charming anthropomorphic Latin engravings. Kate's says, 'That holy man, James Kennedy, Bishop of St Andrews and founder of the College of the Holy Saviour, had me cast in the year 1460 giving me the name of Katharine.' Her companion says, 'I am Elizabeth of St Leonard's cast at Ghent 200 years before and impaired by the ravages of time.' I am beginning to know how she feels.

The quad of St Salvator's – through the arched gate of the Tower – is reminiscent of an Oxford College, with the added bonus that behind you is St Salvator's Chapel, as fine as anything in St Andrews. What draws you to St Salvator's, apart from its venerable intimacy, is how it effortlessly manages to combine the weird, the wonderful and the downright demented. Take the roof.

The bell tower of St Salvator's rising above the medieval city.

It used to be of a beautiful blue stone until 1773 when James Craig, architect of the New Town in Edinburgh, and one must presume in need of work, persuaded the Professors that, being flat, the roof would one day fall to earth and crush them where they sat. The Professors were duly alarmed and Craig won the contract for 'restoration'. It didn't take him long to discover that the roof was so solid and so well attached to the walls and buttresses that the only way he could remove it was by cutting away the wall head and letting gravity take over. Now I don't suppose you need to be a very well qualified architect to appreciate that a solid stone ceiling is heavy, and letting it descend unimpeded, and in one piece, is not a terrific idea. Nevertheless the appropriate incisions were made by workmen who I hope had the foresight to plug their ears with whatever was the 18th century equivalent of cotton wool, and the mighty stone roof hit the ground 'with a crash that shook the whole city'.[89] The Chapel, and particularly the wonderful tomb of its founder, Bishop James Kennedy, was never quite the same again,

Kennedy (1408-65) had many claims to fame besides being the founder of St Salvator's College. He was a Bishop, the Chancellor of the University, and in charge of the government of Scotland for the last five years of his life.* He was described as 'the most distinguished Scotsman of his age', which puts him right up there in the Billy Connolly category. He also had the priceless advantage of minting his own coins and, while for anybody else this would have occasioned an appearance in front of the local magistrates on a charge of forgery, not so for Kennedy, who had been awarded the privilege in 1452 by a grateful Sovereign.[90] No doubt assisted by his own private treasury, Kennedy donated the University's ceremonial mace (as fine a medieval treasure as any university can boast), and owned a barge called *Salvator*, 'the biggest that had been seen to sail upon the Ocean'. (Unfortunately this was wrecked off Bamburgh in 1473 and plundered by the English.)[91]

---

* The young King James III had come to the throne in 1460 and, being only nine, was too young to do the job himself. His father, James II, had taken too close an interest in gunnery. This caused him to blow himself up outside Roxburgh Castle, when one of his great cannons, called the 'Lion', exploded.

He also had made for himself a very fancy tomb. In spite of the fact that the fall of the roof did his last resting-place no good at all, it is worth trying to get into the Chapel just to have a look. It is a tremendous slab of black marble, above which is some wonderfully ornate, albeit fractured, stonework looking for all the world like a block of holiday condos on a Mediterranean hillside. This is more or less what it is. It takes its cue from John: 'In my Father's house are many mansions'. For the medieval tomb designer, heaven was an apartment block.

Opposite the tomb is a 16th-century pulpit, taken from the Town Church, but not the one used by John Knox, apparently. On it is a holder which, I believe, used to contain an hour-glass, similar to a large egg-timer. When the sermon began, the timer was turned over and the sand from the upper chamber trickled slowly down into the lower chamber, thus enabling everyone to make their own calculations and place their bets. This information is uncorroborated. I heard it while tagging onto the end of a tour for Asian royalty, conducted by an eminent member of the University, but it deserves to be true if for no other reason than it is just the sort of device that should be fitted to the front of every pulpit. It would stop the congregation looking at its collective watch, and it would test the nerve of any preacher wishing to occupy a second hour. Bending down and reversing the thing could hardly be done surreptitiously. The congregation would notice, and cough.

While we are in the 16th century, you may want to know what the trendy academics of the day were wearing. Was it a corduroy jacket above a discordant pair of corduroy trousers? No. It was more like sensible golfing clothing for a cold day on the links – woolly hat and thick 'clerical' robes with a polo-neck to keep out the wind. I know this because on the right-hand (west) wall as you come into the Chapel is the tombstone of Provost Hugh Spens, who died in 1534. Cut into his tomb is the only illustration that remains of the everyday dress of a Scottish academic in the Middle Ages. Not all of St Salvator's men left such a worthy legacy. Provost William Cranston, for example, the last Provost in post before the 1560 Reformation, was said to have absconded with a large part of the moveable goods of the College which, besides not doing much for the College finances, was apparently not untypical of the standards of the day.[92] Uncertain times offer temptations, and all that. Of course, not every Provost was dishonest, far from it. Some were merely touched. Only this century, Principal Sir James Irvine, while carrying out a series of improvements to St Salvator's, claimed to have received, in a dream, direct guidance from John Knox himself. He was 'instructed' to carve the words 'We know that even if our earthly home is destroyed, God's heavenly building is eternal'* above the entrance to the Chapel Choir.[93] While this gnomic formula may have been of some comfort to the ghost of the architect who demolished the roof, it does also suggest that a certain caution is in order when it comes to transcribing midnight revelations into stone. Principal Irvine would have done well to pay heed to a story told by William James.[94] This concerned a man who, when under the influence of laughing gas, knew the secret of the universe – but, when he came to, could never remember what it was. At last, with immense effort, he managed to write down the secret before the vision faded. As soon as he woke up, he rushed to see what he had written. The words read: 'A smell of petroleum prevails throughout.'

The next college to be founded in St Andrews, after St Salvator's, was St Leonard's in 1512. Before South Street reaches the Pends, there is a lane to the right which leads into what was then St Leonard's College and is now St Leonards School, one of the first private schools in the country to provide a boarding education for girls. Since St Leonard is the patron saint of prisoners and pregnant women, change of use to a girls' boarding school may have been entirely appropriate. The buildings and grounds are attractive and the old Chapel, which still remains part of the University, is from time to time (according to a timetable I have never managed to unravel) open to the public. To look round the school, you may have to pretend to be a prospective parent.

Being a student in the early days of St Leonard's College was no picnic. A strict code of conduct[95] applied and every hour of the day

* From 2 Cor. 5:1. The words inscribed in the Chapel are in Latin.

On the importance of choosing the right father – and spectacles

The founder* of St Leonard's College was Alexander Stewart who was about as wonderful, as tragic and as pathetic as they come. Alexander Stewart was born in 1493 (probably), the illegitimate son of James IV. By 1502, at the age of nine, he was an Archdeacon. In 1504, having reached the ripe old age of 11, he was Archbishop of St Andrews.[96] Cynics have argued that it may not have been sheer talent alone that caused this stunning advance but could have had a little to do with Dad's desire to keep clerical patronage and revenues in the family. Be that as it may, he doesn't seem to have performed too badly and certainly did not neglect his books. In 1509, he studied under Erasmus, the renowned Dutch scholar and humanist, who called him 'a pupil most promising versatile and accomplished'. By 1513, at the age of 20, Stewart was dead, fighting and dying alongside his father at the battle of Flodden, when the largest army ever led into battle by a Scottish King was slaughtered by the English. Well, you might say, death comes to us all and at least he died with his boots on. Except that it turns out that he was as blind as a bat and would have stood on the battlefield like a helpless baby, unable to see the man who killed him. Erasmus wrote later that Alexander couldn't read a word unless the book was on the end of his nose, literally, in Erasmus' words, touching his nose – *ut ni naso contingeret librum, nihil cerneret.*[97] You might want to pause for a moment and imagine yourself standing on a battlefield hearing the cannon firing around you, the screams of the mutilated and the dying, the march of soldiers approaching – and not being able to see beyond the end of your spear. What do you pray for? A quick death, I suppose, and the courage to stand up straight, face the battle and not to flinch as cold steel penetrates your skin. Erasmus, in a eulogy to the boy, asked what on earth he was doing in the fight. 'Should the scholar take the field, a bishop ride to war?' he wrote. 'Surely it was an exceeding loyalty – for a father imposed this upon thee; and loving thy father all too well, thou wast cut down with him in an unhappy hour.' One hundred years later, Alexander could have worn spectacles. In 1629, Charles I granted a charter to the Spectacle Makers Guild of England and the era of spending two hours a day trying to find the damn things began.

* More precisely, co-founder: with Prior John Hepburn.

had its appropriate duty. Students were told when to get up, when to go to bed, how much food to eat and what to wear. They could speak only Latin and were not allowed out of the College except by special permission. The red gowns that the students wore, and still do, were designed to make them conspicuous so that their misdeeds would come to light. The only woman allowed in College was the laundress and it was specifically stated that she had to be over 50[98] (and presumably past her best). Given that poor working women died young in those days, the students probably ended up doing their own washing. This was the regime that applied to St Leonard's College in 1512 and lived on more or less unchanged in British boarding schools until the 1970s. Duty, strict discipline and no sex was the educational recipe on which the British Empire was built.

The last of the old College foundations is St Mary's (1537), which is about half-way along South Street. Given that its birth occurred in the run-up to the most turbulent period of St Andrews history and between the Plagues of 1529 and 1539, the College is remarkably cosy and comforting. In many ways, it's the most attractive of the University Colleges. The trees help. In front of you, when you come through the arch from South Street, is a spreading 18th-century holm-oak with leaves more like holly than oak, and to the right is a thorn tree planted by the ubiquitous Mary Queen of Scots who obviously found time, between her heroic efforts to park herself on every other piece of furniture in the country, to do a spot of gardening. (MQoS devotees may be interested to know that there is a Queen Mary's bedroom in St Leonards School which, statistically improbable as it may be, appears to be the genuine article.) The original 15th-century buildings are *in situ* on the west side (to the right as you come in), and retain a gnarled charm. You can pick out the coat of arms of Archbishop Hamilton – who finished off the work started by David Beaton – above the entrance to the western stair tower. The building on the north side is called Parliament Hall, because – this may not come as a surprise – it has been used by the Scottish Parliament. The year was 1645, the year of the Great Plague which St Andrews, alone among Scotland's major cities, managed to avoid. Parliament Hall was built in the 1620s and, if you can talk your way in, is rather splendid. If you are young enough, you might pretend to be a student with exams to sit. Otherwise pull strings. The rest of the original quad of St Mary's is no more. The south side used to contain the Common Hall but after about a hundred years, the powers-that-be decided to create a virtual quad by dispensing with the south side altogether. The eastern side was the College Chapel, but was rebuilt first as the old University Library and then as the Psychology Department.

The University, although created by Catholic Bishops and blessed by the Pope, survived 1560 and the triumph of Protestantism in reasonable shape. This was due in no small part to the fact that the University had had the good sense to educate Catholics, Protestants and cloth trimmers alike. No discrimination here. So for every Catholic Beaton, Hamilton or Bishop Reid of Orkney (founder of Edinburgh University) who had gained a degree here, there was a Protestant Hamilton (Patrick), John Major (no, not that one), Melville and Buchanan. Even John Knox himself was an old alumnus (probably) so that when the new brooms started sweeping, the alma mater was left in place. St Andrews had not become the national University of Scotland as originally intended – Aberdeen and Glasgow saw to that – but it was still the dominant centre of higher learning in the country and still Scotland's best production line for turning out scholars, churchmen, jurists, statesmen and poets.[99] Of St Andrews' poets, three of Scotland's finest took their degrees here – William Dunbar in 1479, Gavin Douglas in 1494 and Sir David Lindsay in 1508 – which gives me an excuse to treat you to some of Dunbar's wonderfully morbid lines as he ruminates on how the fear of death troubles him – 'timor mortis conturbat me'.

> Our plesance heir is all vane glory,
> This fals warld is bot transitory,
> The flesche is brukle, the Fend is sle;*
> Timor Mortis conturbat me.
>
> The stait of man dois change and vary,

* The flesh is weak, the Fiend (Devil) is sly.

Now sound, now seik, now blith, now sary,*
Now dansand mery, now like to dee;
Timor Mortis conturbat me.

One to the ded gois all estatis,
Princis, prelotis and potestatis,
Baith riche and pur of al degree:
Timor Mortis conturbat me.

From a man that cannae spell, that's no bad at a'.

After the Reformation, St Andrews hung on in there until 1689, warmed by the occasional reminder of former glories – a brief moment in 1617 when James VI of Scotland (now also James I of England) made a royal visit† and St Andrews was once again the ecclesiastical capital of Scotland and centre of its educational life[100]. But it was a struggle and not to last. After 1689, it was double bogies all round. Doom, gloom and despond. The Stewart Kings had gone. The Presbyterian system of church government was established and out went the Archbishops of St Andrews and its role as ecclesiastical capital, never to return. Trade and industry was moving westward and to the bigger cities. The Act of Union of 1707, which turned Scotland and England into a United Kingdom, pushed the centre of gravity southward. St Andrews' position as a small-town backwater on the east coast of Scotland, in the middle of nowhere, was confirmed. 'This fals warld is bot transitory,' as Dunbar so rightly pointed out.

---

* Now happy, now sad.

† According to Grierson (p. 32), James VI described his return to Scotland as 'a salmon-like instinct to see the place of his breeding'. None of the later Stewart Kings even made this much effort, unless you count the attempts by the Old and Young Pretenders to reclaim the thorne in 1715 and 1745.

CHAPTER 9

The University: fall and rise

IN 1696, A UNIVERSITY servant violently attacked a poor unsuspecting citizen of the town and, on being apprehended, was summoned to appear before the Burgh court. He didn't show up, so the court fined him for contempt. At this point the university stepped in and made it known that, according to its ancient privileges, it had the right to deal with this matter itself – whereupon all hell broke loose and town and gown spent the next two years at each other's throats.[101] The town brought cannon up to the College gates, while the students 'conceived the spirited project of burning down the town'.[102] The University Chancellor of the day, the Earl of Tullibardine, decided that one way to resolve the matter was to up sticks and move lock, stock and barrel to Perth. He commissioned a report, subsequently shelved, but interesting reading nonetheless. St Andrews, it said, is remote. Epidemics flourish on the herring guts which litter the streets. The food is expensive, and other necessities unobtainable. The water is virtually undrinkable and the air 'thin and piercing' so that old men visiting were 'instantly cut off'.* The inhabitants, the report continued, are argumentative, coarse and prone to take advantage and, worst of all, can't stand the Professors – a feeling which was entirely reciprocated. The Professors complained that the town was such a poor shopping centre, that they had to go to Edinburgh to buy their 'hattes'.[103] (Why does this sound familiar?) As St Andrews stood on the cusp of the 18th century, not everything in its garden was rosy. In fact, most of it was uneatable, undrinkable or generally injurious to health and friendship.

After that, things really started to go downhill. Fifty years

---

* I presume this means that old men were cut off from their oxygen supply, but it may be that they were cut off at the knees by being pierced repeatedly. There have been days when I have felt like that.

later, with the buildings crumbling and student numbers falling, the university decided to rationalise. St Salvator's and St Leonard's were amalgamated and the St Leonard's buildings were sold to one Robert Watson for £200 plus £10 a year.[104] Not a bad buy, considering that this now comprises much of the land and buildings of St Leonards School. The Church of St Leonard's wasn't sold, partly because it wasn't clear who owned it, but this didn't save it from becoming a ruin. The roof was removed, the church bell transferred to St Salvator's, and the rest left to rot quietly (until 1910, when restoration began). By the 1790s, it wasn't just the buildings that were in decay. The moral structure was also starting to fray. At one point, George Hill, Principal of St Mary's College, managed to ensure that six out of thirteen members of the University's governing body were relations of his.[105] One more and he could have decided all university business over breakfast. Psalm 121 was understandably popular amongst University staff at that time: 'I will lift up mine eyes unto the Hills, from whence cometh my help.'[106]

The 19th century wasn't a heck of a lot better. There were good intentions and some rebuilding but no reversal of the steady decline. In the 1870s, student numbers were 130, compared to 2,375 at Edinburgh, 1,775 at Glasgow and 680 in Aberdeen.[107] No wonder golf was the University game. To have organised a game of football, 17% of the University would have had to have shown up, excluding the referee. Then, magically and mysteriously in the way these things do, the up-swing started. University College was established in Dundee and bolted on to St Andrews (now unbolted). Government funding increased, bequests came in, facilities improved and some talented professors recruited. So much so that, by the early 20th century, the University was back in business.

As we enter the 21st century, we find that the patient has climbed off his deathbed, kissed goodbye to the nurses and been swinging about with his walking stick to such good effect that some elements are starting to wonder if they didn't prefer the old days. As you drive into St Andrews on the A91, the large acreage on the right is crawling with some of the most unattractive concrete blocks, masquerading as science buildings, you are ever likely to see – although you could go down to the East Sands and gaze at the student accommodation there that the University has seen fit to lumber us with. Where is planning permission when we need it? The number of students in town, to say nothing of their cars, has been rising consistently and reached some 5,000 at the last count, many of whom are golfers and in danger of swamping the courses. But that is life. One moment it is famine, the next feast.

St Andrews and the American Declaration of Independence

Even when St Andrews University was just about at rock bottom, it still managed to cling to the coat-tails of world affairs. Three of its alumni, Benjamin Franklin, John Witherspoon and James Wilson, were signatories of the 1776 Declaration of Independence – which, I imagine, is something no other university in the world can boast. Franklin was awarded his LL.D. degree in 1758,[108] years before he signed the Declaration, but after he had taken the novel step of attaching a metal key to a kite, and holding on to it during a lightning storm, thus proving that lightning is electrical energy. The LL.D. was probably for bravery. Witherspoon was a Scottish Presbyterian Minister from East Lothian, who went on to become the first President of Princeton University and to spend a large part of his time urging Americans to speak properly.* To no avail, obviously. James Wilson was a local boy made good – a Fifer by birth (from Caskerdo farm, near Ceres,) and a student at St Andrews from 1757 to 1762. After moving to America in 1765, he became one of only six people to sign both the Declaration of Independence and the Constitution of the USA. His brief spell in jail for injudicious property speculation could not be blamed on his alma mater.

* Witherspoon wrote a number of articles in the *Pennysylvania Journal and Weekly Advertiser* in which he attacked the linguistic 'improperties and vulgarisms' of his fellow Americans.

One reason out of many (somewhere in the bottom half of a long list), why the flickering candle of university life wasn't entirely snuffed out, was that the University has been well served by its Rectors, two of whom, the Marquess of Bute and Andrew Carnegie, were particularly rich and generous. Originally, in the early 1400s, it was the Rector who ran the show, but in modern times (since 1858), the Rector has been somebody who has been chosen by the students to act both as their representative and as

Chairman of the University Court. (To let the students choose the Chairman of the Board sounds like an act of unadulterated lunacy but, remarkably, it seems to have worked.) The Rector is not to be confused with the Chancellor, who is the titular head of the University, nor with the Principal, who is the man who really runs the University day to day. Glad we cleared that up.

The Rectors were a mixed bunch ranging from writers such as J. M. Barrie and Rudyard Kipling, to Earl Haig, the First World War general, who was actually invited to stand (and accepted) in 1916 when one might have thought he had a few other things on his mind (such as sending a million soldiers to their death in the trenches). Many famous men have stood for election and failed such as Benjamin Disraeli, T. H. Huxley, and Sean Connery. Arthur Conan Doyle and Mussolini were nominated but did not make the short list. No Screaming Lord Sutch. There is a story that one of the gateways in the town (though nobody knows quite which) will crumble when a true genius passes underneath. When the philosopher John Stuart Mill became Rector (1865-8), he noticed that the Rectorial Drag* traditionally passed through the West Port, the ancient gateway at the western end of South Street. He refused to go through it, no doubt terrified that it would not fall down. No other Rector has suffered from quite such presumption and the West Port still stands – and is worth close inspection. (Just watch out that you are not squashed by passing cars as you step back to admire King David I wielding his spear.)

After his inauguration, Mill never showed up to University meetings but the 3rd Marquess of Bute (1892-98) did. Bute[109] was certainly generous, a quality which endeared him greatly to the University, as did his support for the Students' Union and the Medical School which bears his name. Besides being a benefactor, Bute had some dramatic ideas. One was to rebuild the western end of the Cathedral with funding from his noble friends who would, in return, be allowed to carve their coats of arms into the walls. This was in the 19th century when Coca Cola and corporate spon-

---

* This is the name given to the ceremony in which a new Rector is hauled around the town by his students. The Rector remains appropriately attired.

sorship were still ideas whose time had not yet come. Then there was his approach to the problem of Butts Wynd, the lane that runs from St Salvator's to The Scores – it wasn't wide enough for his carriage. Solution: widen the lane. Lesser men would have acquired a narrower carriage. Bute, among his other attributes, had the capacity to be gloriously and unconcernedly rude. When all the members of the University Court retired to Rusacks Marine Hotel for lunch after their meetings, twelve of them would sit on one table while Bute, who couldn't stand Principal Donaldson, would dine on a separate table of his own. I imagine Donaldson got the point.

The other great Rectorial benefactor was Andrew Carnegie (1901-07),[110] a Fifer from Dunfermline, and one of the richest men in the world. Such was his fortune, made in the American steel industry, that, by the time he died, he had reputedly given away in one way or another and in one place or another over $300m, which was a tidy sum in those days. This was the kind of Rector that St Andrews appreciated and he provided for the library, and for scholarships, playing fields and other benefactions. There was talk that the University conned Carnegie into funding a new organ for St Salvator's Chapel, but pay no heed. Carnegie was positively fetishistic in his love for bequeathing organs (musical) and managed to do so on a magnificent 7,689 occasions in his lifetime. This is a large number of organs by any standards. Now let us assume he got rid of one every day of the year including Christmas, it would still take him twenty-one years to hand out 7,689, and any man who is this dedicated does not have to be conned. I imagine the first syllable, 'org', had scarcely left the Principal's lips before Carnegie had him discussing delivery dates. Since Carnegie, the list of Rectors has included Nansen the explorer, Jan Smuts, Marconi, Sir Learie Constantine, John Cleese and Frank Muir, and few have been better than the last two for dedication and a capacity to entertain. The current Rector is Andrew Neil.

The University's revival has certainly been helped by its ability to recruit first-rate academics. People like living here. That good and kindly man, Earl Haig, when offered the post of Chancellor, declared that he would 'accept anything that will take me back to St Andrews'. Over the years, some talented men and women have been lured here, but none has been regarded more highly than Professor Sir D'Arcy Thompson (1860-1948), thought by some to be the greatest polymath of this century. To attract D'Arcy to St Andrews, it is said that the University offered him the choice of a professorial chair in Classics, Mathematics or Zoology, and he chose Zoology. His book *On Growth and Form* is where science meets Greek and, if you like to wallow in intricate, erudite and beautifully constructed sentences, you will usually find a copy in one of the town's second-hand bookshops. The etching on the plaque outside his house at 44 South Street is only intelligible to those who have read the book, and I am not about to try to summarise it – partly because I never made it past Chapter 1. D'Arcy's bust and much of the physical material discussed in the book are on display in the Bell-Pettigrew Museum,* along with a page from his commentary on Greek fishes: labelled, I should tell you, in Latin, Greek, Egyptian, Arabic and Coptic. Actually, you should go and see the Bell-Pettigrew anyway, if for no other reason than it demonstrates that the entire world's population can probably stand, side by side, on the Isle of Wight. Into a room large enough to allow an average family to watch television in comfort, has been crammed just about every species that has ever walked, crawled, swum or flown across this earth. There are Dodo bones, the hind leg of a Diplodocus, a flying Lemur, an Indian Anteater, fossils, marsupials, centipedes and segmented worms. There is even a Wapiti head, shot by Captain, later General, Playfair, RA. The space is so densely populated that you have to move around with the precision of a brain surgeon entering a frontal lobe. Don't, for heavens sake, cough, or the floor will be strewn with camel bones and the pickled remains of a urochordata (aka sea squirt).

D'Arcy, I imagine, was at home in the B-P. He was an eccentric. One of his favoured pastimes was walking round St Andrews with a coruscating and conversational parrot on his shoulder.

---

* Part of the Bute Building, on Queen's Terrace.

Today, this sort of behaviour might be vulnerable to the odd remark. I remember when the Babur, a rather splendid Indian restaurant (now deceased) opened in South Street, the owner had the imaginative idea of dressing up his younger brother in full tribal regalia – ceremonial headgear, tulwar, the lot – and having him stand in the street to drum up business. Unfortunately the restaurant was next door to the Criterion Bar (also now deceased) which was a drinking house that took its drinking seriously. As the drinkers staggered blinking out of the Crit into the winter's evening and cast about them to get their bearings, they found themselves eyeball to eyeball with a Kashmiri warrior freezing to death. This came as a profound shock to both parties and it wasn't long before the young Indian was withdrawn to safety, indoors. Which all goes to show that eccentricity, however harmless, is easily knocked off its perch. D'Arcy's parrot would have understood.

CHAPTER 10

The Burgh

A PRESENT-DAY RESIDENT jumping aboard a time-machine and alighting in medieval St Andrews would, broadly speaking, feel at home. Seeing the Cathedral and the Castle in their pristine state might come as a surprise (a pleasant one, I imagine), and he might wonder at the cart-loads of clerics on every street corner, but the layout of the old town would look more or less as he had left it in the 21st century. No planners in those days, so the building style would have been attractively random – some houses fronting onto the street, some gable-end on,* and many, at least until the mid-16th century, timber-framed, thatched and forever burning down. Many of the stone houses had outside staircases† and the larger ones then, as now, had cellars at the bottom and living quarters on the first floor above the street: the better to look out on the world below. However, what might have startled our man would have been the fabulous beasts – camels, lemurs, crocodiles, parakeets and other exotica – painted on the walls of the houses of this con-servative northern city.** And all this before Bell-Pettigrew was a twinkle in his father's eye.

It might take our traveller a moment or two to put his finger on what he didn't see as he promenaded down South Street or Market Street. No shops for one thing: no medieval equivalent of Woolworths or Boots. People bought what they needed from booths at a weekly market at the Market Cross†† or from the big

---

* A good example is 10 Argyle Street which is unaltered today.

† As you can still see at 19 North Street, 15 South Castle Street and elsewhere.

** Jurek Pütter, diligently digging through bills of lading from the Dutch Maritime Museum, has unearthed details of animal pattern books and templates flooding in from Flanders. The elephant, as befits its size, arrived here in four pieces and the giraffe in two – body and legs, and neck – but the neck was reversible (so the animal could look forward or back).

†† In Market Street (more or less at the intersection with Church Street).

Cautionary Tale (2)

One curious feature of the old houses was that the chimneys were festooned with sharp spikes (rather than chimney pots as now). These were to prevent birds from falling down and flapping around inside, but the flip side was that they posed serious risks to the unwary. Consider, for example, the case of the unfortunate sweep, the Ebony Boy of Edinburgh. Whilst going about his business some 400 years ago, he had the bad luck to fall foul of a set of chimney spikes, on which he remained impaled, aloft and unnoticed, for a year. When he was finally discovered and brought down to earth, he was found to have been perfectly preserved – in fact, smoked, (like a kipper). He was then, in the true spirit of free enterprise, exhibited.*

*This story was told to me by Jurek Pütter, who is a reliable source. The references are lost, however, so believe or not. Don't doubt though that those who slipped up on society's roof tops came to a sticky end.

---

annual fairs. No noxious, pole-axing stench either which, if he had been watching BBC costume dramas or had any knowledge of St Andrews' more recent past, he might have expected. Things were to become immeasurably worse by the late 1600s but, in the Middle Ages, St Andrews, as a great pilgrim city, probably had drainage and some paving.[111] The drainage system was accidentally rediscovered in the mid-19th century when a horse and cart, clip-clopping down Abbey Street, broke through the surface and fell into a medieval culvert.[112] The cart was quickly removed, but the horse was left with its head and body underground, while its tail stuck out like a flag of truce. This was too much for the local youth, who amused themselves by pulling out the poor creature's waving hairs one by one. By the time it was finally extricated (alive, amazingly), its rear end had become its scrag end, and quite possibly its bitter end.

The thing that our voyager couldn't fail to spot was that people dressed a bit differently in those days. If a fellow ponced up to you in a close-fitting doublet, with 'hose' (stockings) and a pleated ruff, I think you'd notice. He'd be a nobleman.[113] The merchants, a rung or two lower on the social ladder, went about their business in a puffy tunic, red stockings (probably), and with a handbag swinging temptingly from a silk belt. (These merchants were

The Market Gate in 1525 (which survived until 1827).
The picture also shows James V's camel, on tour.

attached to their hats apparently, which they wore indoors and out and, according to the miniaturists of the period, in bed.)[114] The citizens of low estate, however, were generally prevented from wearing anything other than plain grey homespun. As an editorial note to those still reeling from the fact that medieval St Andrews was able to survive without shops, I would point out that if you have to wear homespun, i.e. cloth that is spun at home, the need for clothes shops is somewhat reduced.

In the Middle Ages, everyone in St Andrews more or less knew their place. They didn't always like it but, since so much depended on inherited rank and privilege, there wasn't a great deal most people could do about their lot in life except pray to be born lucky. On that score, you could do a great deal worse than turn up on life's doorstep as a St Andrews' merchant. One of the peculiarities of a royal burgh, such as St Andrews, was that only merchants were allowed to buy and sell goods abroad, or indeed up and down the coast. All the other townsmen had to confine their activities to the town boundaries and, even then, couldn't trade in expensive goods such as fish, hides and wool.[115] In other words, the merchants had a monopoly on all the entrepreneurial activities (outside the Church) that were likely to make serious money – with predictable consequences. The merchants became rich* and the rest of the town became jealous. Riots were frequent and the have-nots, in order to pursue war by other means, set up a few restrictive practices of their own, namely the craft organisations.† The most important of these were the thunderously named 'Hammermen', who were in fact an amalgam of blacksmiths, armourers, wheelwrights, saddlers, glovers, dyers, clothmakers, goldsmiths, cutlers, pewterers and lorimers[116] (who made metal

---

* On top of the easy pickings from trade, merchants were generally able to command a seat on the Town Council, which brought with it the opportunity for any number of corrupt practices. The virulent plague of 1585 provided one example of the kind of things they got up to. First, the Councillors levied a tax ostensibly to help the plague victims and then, when the money arrived, trousered it. After which, they either seized the estates of the poor unfortunates who had perished, or levied an inheritance tax on the grieving offspring.

† The craft organisations in St Andrews were the hammermen, the wrights, the baxters, the tailors, the cordiners, the weavers and the fleshers.

accessories for horses – ashtrays, drink holders, that sort of thing).
Part of the point of the crafts was to keep out the even less
fortunate, a group of people known as the 'unfreemen'* who, as
their name suggests, were not greatly endowed with life's privileges.
In fact they didn't have any, and not much in the way of civil rights
either.[117] Medieval Scotland, in case you hadn't guessed, was not
big on that kind of thing.

One thing that did unite the citizens, great and small, was the
town church, Holy Trinity. It seems to have begun life in 1144[118]
as part of the Cathedral complex, but moved to its present site in
South Street in 1412. From then on, it was always part of the town
in a way that the Cathedral was not. The merchants and craft
organisations even dipped into their own pockets to keep it in
good repair[119]. Compared to the Cathedral, which was immensely
grand, Holy Trinity was home, somewhere where you could take
your boots off and let your hair down, in neither case literally of
course. It was where the town gathered to hear John Knox preach
on those fateful days in June 1559, when all present agreed to
remove 'idolatrie' and deliver to the medieval Church the unam-
biguous message that its time was up. It was from Holy Trinity
that the mob set forth to wreck the Cathedral, though what they
thought of their handiwork after the looting was over, who can
tell? Pleasure that the days of Protestant bonfires and Catholic
excesses were over? Regret that, in the grimmer and harsher climate
that was to follow, the new kirk sessions would come down hard
on the harmless frivolities and gentle pleasures, golf included, that
had been enjoyed for centuries? Probably both. In any event, Holy
Trinity survived the Reformation sparser, but intact, and was only
brought low by disastrous rebuilding in 1798, partially reversed†
in the 1900s.[120] What remains of the original of 1412 is the tower,
part of the west wall and a number of the pillars on the north side.

---

* The unfreemen worked as labourers on the land, at sea or in the houses of the better-off.

† The Church was restored using designs that were comparable to those that would have
been used in the 15th century. It was a sign of changing times that the designs included
two niches of St Salvator proportions for statues and that the masons were allowed to dec-
orate the walls with animal carvings. Very un-Presbyterian.

The building is a recommended tourist stomping-ground and the tour should probably begin with a stroll around the outside of the church. Holy Trinity backs onto Church Square which, in spite of also housing the public lavatory, is a delight. On sunny days, it strikes me that it has the feel of a small Italian piazza, although this may be the first symptom of cabin fever after a long winter. Inside the church, Douglas Strachan's stained glass windows are outstanding as, in its own way, is the huge marble monument recording one of the most violent episodes in St Andrews history – the murder of Archbishop Sharp in 1679.

Sharp was an accident waiting to happen but, even so, he was a touch unlucky to be bumped off in the way he was. His murderers began the morning of Friday 2 May with another target in mind, one William Carmichael, the sheriff depute of Fife, when news reached them that the coach of the Archbishop of St Andrews, who was Primate of all Scotland and one of King Charles II's Privy Councillors, was on its way from Kennoway to St Andrews.[121] This was a more splendid catch altogether, and nine men, Covenanters* all, led by the Lairds Hackston and Balfour, mounted their horses and chased the coach down. They drew level with it at Magus Muir,† opened the door, dragged Sharp out, and stabbed him in the kidneys and above his right eye. They then split his skull and rode away. The screams of his daughter, Isabel, who had been travelling with her father and forced to witness this gruesome mutilation, were heard half a mile away.[122]

Of the nine men** who set out after Sharp that day, only two, Hackston and Guillan were brought to justice, even though the authorities knew just about everything there was to know about the murderers, up to and including what they had had for breakfast.

* The Covenant was a political manifesto declaring the supremacy of Parliament and Presbytery over King and Bishops.

† Magus Muir is by Strathkiness, a few miles from St Andrews. The old coach road no longer exists.

** The nine were: two lairds, David Hackston of Rathillet, John Balfour of Kinloch; six tenant farmers, James Russell, George Fleming, Alexander and Andrew Henderson, William Dingwall and George Balfour; and one weaver, Andrew Guillan.

The Road to Retribution

In his early years, James Sharp had been a staunch Presbyterian. He had no doubt that the last thing the Church needed was bishops, particularly bishops who were little better than intermediaries of the King. He won his spurs as a talented negotiator for the Scottish Presbyterians in their dealings with Cromwell, and his career was set fair. Then along came one of those nightmare choices that makes all men of ambition start up in the middle of the night, lathered in sweat. In 1660 Charles II was restored to the monarchy, and it soon became clear to all that Presbyterianism was out and bishops were back. What was poor Sharp to do? Stay true to his principles and retire from the political arena, or persuade himself that he should work with the new system in order to soften its worst effects? Sharp, like other men in public life before and since, opted for the latter and was rewarded with the plum appointment of Archbishop of St Andrews. His erstwhile colleagues were not pleased, and became even less pleased as Sharp found it easier and easier with each passing year to forget the things he once believed in. By the end, he was widely seen across Scotland as little more than an agent of England, a champion of episcopacy and an apologist for the supremacy of royal power.[123] This did not make him the most popular fellow ever to set foot in Hibernia, and he was variously described as a schemer, greedy, devious and 'the greatest knave that ever was in the Church of Scotland'[124] – which was quite an accolade. Retribution caught up with him on Magus Muir.

For one thing, the murder took place in broad daylight and the coachmen, who saw exactly what happened, lived to tell the tale. For another, the murderers were in no hurry to cover their tracks. They left Magus Muir 'riding less hastily than when they had come', and made their way to the home of James Anderson, a tenant farmer near Largo who, as soon as they had left, spilt the beans by the bucket load. It didn't make any difference. In spite of all this, and the offer of a large reward, Hackston was only picked up somewhat by accident in 1680 after the Covenanting forces had been defeated at Airds Moss. His end was gruesome. His hands were cut off. He was then hung, dismembered and forced to endure the posthumous indignity of having his various bits put on display in St Andrews, Glasgow, Leith and Burntisland. In a macabre postscript, one of Hackston's hands is buried in Cupar churchyard,* eleven miles from St Andrews. The headstone carries a picture of the grave's occupants – a right hand and two heads which had been previously attached, not to Hackston himself as his detractors might have supposed, but separately to two Covenanters, Lawrence Hay and Andrew Pitulloch, neither of whom had had anything to do with the murder. The idea of interring miscellaneous body parts in one grave is unusual in modern Scotland, but then, these days, we tend to croak intact. Whilst my own preference is for cremation (and then to be scattered, preferably from a low-flying aircraft, over the Old Course along with the remains of thousands of other golfers who have left similar bequests),† I wouldn't object if my kids, before consigning me to the furnace, wished to cut off an appendage – a big toe perhaps – and bury that separately. And I would be happy to share my hole in the ground. Others' parts could join me. A few legs here, a few arms there and pretty soon we would have enough to make grave robbers of the future muse about the damage genetically modified foods must have done to my generation.

If you are in need of a gentle diversion from St Andrews, you might think of a triangular tour, setting off for the Magus Muir monuments, on to Cupar and back to the magnificent Sharp memorial in Holy Trinity. Magus Muir is now a wood off an unnamed road that joins the B939 above Strathkiness, so you might want to ratchet up the odds of success by buying the Ordnance Survey map (59) of St Andrews before setting out. When you arrive at the sign that says 'to the monuments', take the left-hand path through the wood. This leads to a stone marking the spot where five Covenanters were hanged to appease the Archbishop's ghost. These poor unfortunates had no discernible connection to the murder but, since the government hadn't been able to lay its hands on the real killers, somebody had to swing.

---

* I am unable to shed light on how, precisely, it found its way to Cupar from its initial resting place beneath the Edinburgh gibbet.

† The Road Hole bunker on the 17th is a favoured resting-place and you may notice that the sand there is of a somewhat paler complexion and lighter consistency than elsewhere.

And they were Covenanters, after all. Close by is a miniature pyramid, looking more like a stone beehive than anything else, commemorating Sharp. You might want to walk back up the road to Claremont Farm to find the memorial to Andrew Guillan, or alternatively take the road to Ceres and then turn off to Cupar. The old graveyard is a peaceful place, the church is worth seeing and the memorial to Hackston's hand, close by the Ashlar Lane wall, is not too difficult to find. The headstone reads:

> Here lies interred the Heads of Laur'ce Hay and Andrew Pitulloch who suffered martyrdom . . . for adhering to the word of God, & Scotland's covenanted work of Reformation, and also one of the Hands of David Hackston who was most cruelly murdered . . . for the same cause.

If you want to make a day trip out of this tour, take the bus. Ever vigilant on your behalf, Andrew (offspring no 3) and I went down to the bus station (just beyond the west end of Market Street) to enquire about routes. When you reach the office, I wouldn't recommend the approach, straightforward though it is, which begins, 'please could you tell me which bus goes to Magus Muir?' We tried that (on your behalf). No obvious sign of comprehension results. And don't even dream of elaborating. Trust me on this. Best to take a map, and point. The girl behind the desk, whose skills clearly lay elsewhere, passed the matter over to a more cartologically-inclined colleague who could not have been more helpful. As a result, I now know that you need the 64 bus via Craigton Park. This goes past Magus Muir and on to Cupar, but you might want to bear in mind that the interval between buses is two hours, and for reasons I won't go into, the stop for getting off at the monuments is not the same as the stop for getting on. I would be inclined to take the bus driver to one side before you leave St Andrews and discuss all this with him. You might also fortify yourself with the thought that if Lewis and Clark could find their way across the hitherto unexplored western territories of the USA without any knowledge of cartography or native Indian languages, you should be able to get yourself to Cupar and back. At least the natives are friendly and speak a lingo with some similarities to your own.

Ten years after Sharp, a new King (William of Orange) banished the bishops from Scotland and St Andrews continued on its relentless career towards obscurity. Dilapidation was everywhere to be seen. In 1728, of the 945 houses in town, 159 were in ruins.[125] I make that 17%. The impression of decay will not have been helped by some odd University customs. One of these was for the Porter of St Leonard's College, at the beginning of each term, to collect five shillings from each student for the windows he might break. The money was never returned whether or not any damage was done so, at the end of term, the students enjoyed their final hours in College by smashing all the glass they could find.[126] This story was unearthed by Andrew Lang* from *Poems* 1797, written by a St Andrews alumnus, George Berkeley, with a preface by the editor (Mr Berkeley's mother). The poems occupy 212 pages, the preface 630. That is some mother. Lang passes on assorted observations emanating from said Mrs Berkeley, such as that most of the stone houses in South Street were 'disfigured by what is termed a forestair, that is an open staircase (running) in a zigzag manner across the front of the house, and a huge dunghill in front.'[127] Mrs B. goes on to review, at length, various incidents in the life of her son, including one about how he paid the food bills for a poor student who had only a 'a large tub of oatmeal and a pot of salted butter on which to subsist between 20 October and 20 May', the boy's father having sold one of his three cows to send him to St Andrews. Other stories relate to George's parties with mysterious young ladies all dressed in white, duels with an English student who called him a coward and run-ins with 'wonderfully saucy and surly' shopkeepers of the town. Finally Lang, having slogged his way through all 630 pages of Mrs Berkeley's preface, concludes with these well-chosen words: 'These are all the scraps

---

* Andrew Lang was a famous St Andrean, historian and man of letters, who is commemorated in St Salvator's Chapel. He has over 200 books under his name in the British Library as well as numerous co-authorships and joint publications. The term 'prolific' hardly does him justice. His history of St Andrews was published in 1893.

about St Andrews which analysis can extract from a prodigious mass of prattle, the most disjointed chat ever offered by a fond mother to the world.'[128]

It wasn't until the middle of the 19th century that the pendulum swung and the town woke up to the fact that there were alternatives to dilapidated buildings, disease-ridden water supplies and unpaved streets. 'Public works' raised its various heads. Sanitation arrived. Dead horses were no longer left by the side of the road to rot down. Street lighting appeared* so that, on your way back from the public house on a black and windswept evening, you no longer had to trip over the aforementioned horse, and flounder around in its rancid carcass before returning to the bosom of your family. The streets were paved, and police commissioners were elected to ensure an orderly passage along them.[129] The railway reached town in 1852† and, for the local builders, it was boom time in Shangri-La. They went at it flat out, putting up new buildings and tearing down old ones. Much of this construction was sparked by the hyper-active Provost of St Andrews, Sir Hugh Lyon Playfair. The old Tolbooth in Market Street, which had served the town over the centuries as, variously, town hall, tax collection point, police cell, debtors prison, and hustings, was pulled down in 1862 – which was a pity if only because it had character and, if preserved, would have enlarged the provenance of the old town. Sir Hugh, in his self-appointed role as 'new broom', swept away the traditional forestairs and projecting porches of the old houses, and there were 'strange tales told of his arbitrary acts and of assaults on St Leonard's Chapel'. As Andrew Lang puts it, 'Sir Hugh Playfair found St Andrews picturesque and left it clean, or cleaner than its ancient and fishlike wont, . . . (but) much is gone; much that was old and might have been made clean.'[130]

Not, mind you, that the 19th-century additions were all bad, far from it. The streets built at the north west end of the old town – Hope Street, Howard Place and Abbotsford Crescent – have a classical elegance about them. A bit like Bath, looked at through

* Lighting was first by oil, then gas.

† Anyone travelling by train today has to get off at Leuchars, alas.

the wrong end of a telescope. Madras College, opened in 1834 and the largest building to sprout in St Andrews since the Reformation, was described as a 'great blot', but this is a trifle harsh. Appropriately stern, I would say, and well suited to its purpose of educating children. For the first two years of its life, it had no lavatories – which could only have been possible for kids whose forbears had been used to sitting through Knox's sermons. As soon as lavatories were put in, in 1836, the pupils were forbidden to bring firearms to school,[131] though why the one should have prompted the other is far from clear. The School itself is not called Madras because the Head Master believed that a hot curry at lunchtime would fire up his pupils. If it had been, a full suite of ablution facilities would have had to have been provided at the outset. In fact, it is named after the Madras system of education that the school's founder, Dr Andrew Bell,* had developed while in India, whereby older children helped to teach younger. While on site, you will notice, in front of Madras, the polygonal remains of a 16th-century Chapel of the Dominican Friars. The Chapel is a ruin because the Blackfriars, so called because of the colour of their habit, made it one of their prime functions to root out heresy. This, as followers of the Cathedral saga will know, was a sure-fire way of making enemies who, when the appointed hour arrived, would delight in reducing your living quarters to rubble. Which is what happened. It is rather an attractive ruin, particularly when lit at night, and best seen by standing with your back to the school. When I last paused to look, the pupils (if indeed it was them) had demonstrated their appreciation of the view by adorning the Chapel with toffee wrappers, cigarette ends and other miscellaneous accoutrements of modern life.

The Scots are endearingly cautious. If you happen to remark that it's lovely weather, be prepared for a retort along the lines of, 'Aye, but it'll pish doon the morra'. Even so, there must have been a moment, sometime before the end of the 19th century, when the townspeople looked at each other and exchanged a muted, but eloquent, glance along the lines of 'Hey, Jimmy, this toon's gaunae

---

* Bell Street, which runs at 90 degrees to the school, is named after the good Doctor.

be a' richt'. The fact was that the nightmare was over. The years of decline had come to an end. The industrial revolution, and the blight which that had put on so many British cities, had passed St Andrews by. The water had become clean. The air was fresh. The medieval town was largely intact, and, butting on to it were the old Links whose seductive charms were about to be noticed the whole world over. The town could smell the pilgrims saddling up.

We know what happened. The nostrils did not lie. Stagecoach after metaphorical stagecoach piled in and, as the 20th century wore on, the town boundaries stretched ever further south and west. Nevertheless, the auld toun has managed to retain an allure that is not, in my opinion, to be found elsewhere in Britain. Andrew Lang says that the time to see St Andrews is 'not in summer, among crowds of holiday-making strangers, but, in winter, when the scarlet gowns of the students brighten the dim streets, and the waves fill the roofless fanes with their monotone'. Personally, I would say that you would have to be one ice cube short of an igloo to come in winter. Come between May and October, pray for sun, and leave enough time before teeing off to wander our three main streets and the narrow wynds that run between. Go to the Preservation Trust Museum, which is tiny but packed to the gunnels with old photographs* and exhibitions of how it was. Buy yourself a copy of *A Guided Walk round St Andrews* by John Pearson which will fit in your pocket and is on sale at the Information Office. And don't neglect to rise early, when the town is fresh, and retire late. One night, after a quiet drink at the Castle Tavern, we turned into the narrow cobbled end of Market Street. A slight haar lingered against the lights of the street, our shoes clopped on the ancient stones and we peered into the haze that shrouded a thousand years of history. Food for the soul, I thought. Unless it was the beer talking.

---

* St Andrews has a substantial collection of early photographs arising from the part the town played in the early development of photography. Fox-Talbot, who invented Calotype photography in 1839, corresponded with Sir David Brewster, the Principal of the University and a chemist. John Adamson and, subsequently, Robert Adamson and David Hill, and Thomas Rodger took up development of the new techniques in St Andrews. There are early Calotype photographs from 1842.

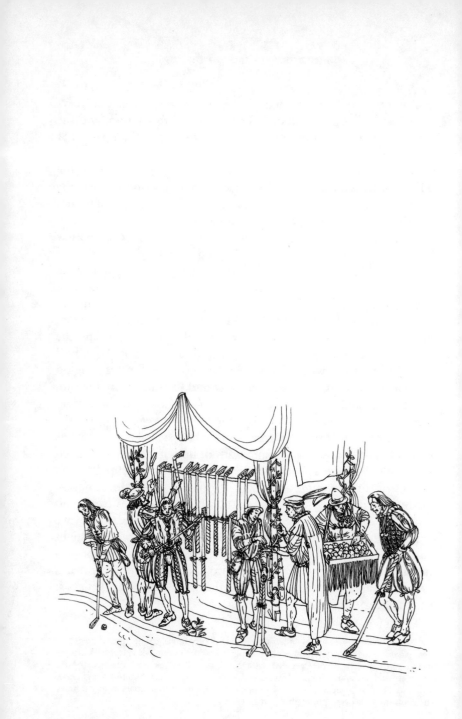

CHAPTER 11

The Links road

ST ANDREWS CLUBMAKERS first came to the notice of the historians in 1672 when a man called Pett supplied golf clubs to the Marquess of Montrose. Then, in the early 1700s, Messrs. Mill and Dick were selling woods to the University students. One hundred years later, Hugh Philp was producing some of the finest clubs ever crafted.[132] Thereafter it became acceptable to have a surname with more than one syllable. Wilson, Forgan and Morris followed and finally, in the full flowering of syllabic profusion, Auchterlonie. These were the great clubmakers, the Eli Calloways of the day, and by Hugh Philp's time, they were centred on the area by the side of what is now the 18th hole and The Links road. This area became the Golf Mall of St Andrews where addicts could wander from workshop to workshop, test the latest prototypes and slip into the 19th hole bar for a wee nip.

Club and ball manufacture was just about the only 'secondary' industry the town had. There was plenty of primary stuff – farming and fishing – and there was the University, but in the sleeves-rolled-up, muck-and-brass sector, golf manufacture was all there was. It played an important part in the town's revival. Hugh Philp's nephew was Robert Forgan who inherited the business in 1856 and, by virtue of an eye for business and an instinct for innovation – most notably the introduction of hickory shafts – expanded it considerably. In the end it employed well over 100 people.[133] This may not sound huge by the standards of General Motors but, even today, would make it just about the town's largest employer outside the University. His main factory was on the site, overlooking the 18th Green, where the R&A offices and ball-testing facilities will be shortly. He also had a cleek-making factory behind 110 Market Street.

Ball-making was in the hands of the caddies and the early professionals. Allan Robertson sold golf balls from the window of his cottage on the corner of Golf Place and the Links, and employed a number of assistants, including Old Tom Morris and the caddie Willie Robertson.

In the Course of Duty

Willie Robertson was known as 'Lang Willie' on account of being six foot two with a liking for tall hats. Willie was typical of the quick-witted St Andrews caddie, always prepared to give as good as he got. Part of the caddies' duties in those days was to take golfers' luggage down to the railway station (in the days when St Andrews had a railway station). On one occasion, Willie was thus employed bearing the luggage of Sir Alexander Kinloch, a future captain of the R&A. He borrowed a barrow from old Tom Morris, (then in charge of the courses) and decided to take the short-cut over the Swilken Bridge. A mistake. His foot struck hard against the bridge and he pitched the whole lot into the water. Kinloch was furious. 'You damned fool! What do you mean . . .', to which Willie turned round and replied coolly, 'Dinna make such a song, Sir Alexander. Be thankful the bags are no' in the Bay of Biscay. They're damned easy to get oot o' the Swilken', and with that he jumped in, reloaded, squelched down to the station and (no doubt grinning quietly to himself) helped Kinloch decant his sopping suitcases onto the train.[134]

Willie was not always in the best of health. According to Richard Mackenzie in his very readable history of the St Andrews caddies,[135] he suffered a stroke whilst out caddying on the golf course. A fellow caddie asked him how he felt. 'I felt naething' he replied. In the morning his sister told him his face looked pale and twisted. 'Nonsense!' cried Willie. Then, as he put it later, 'When I sat doon tae ma porritch, ma jaw widnae work.' He died of a heart attack whilst caddying on the Old Course.

Making balls was lucrative. In 1844, Allan Robertson was reputed to have sold 2,556 featheries[136] and given he could charge about two shillings a ball,[137] this wasn't bad business on top of his competition earnings. Not surprisingly, he didn't immediately welcome the new gutta-percha ball which came in 1848. When he found Tom Morris using it, the two had a falling out, with Morris setting up in competition. In the end, Allan Robertson bowed to the inevitable, starting producing guttas which were simpler to manufacture and, at one shilling a ball, made even more profit. He wasn't the only one. Bob Kirk, a caddie, had a box in Golf Place where he sat every day boiling pieces of gutta in a stew-pan.[138] He would squeeze the boiled mess into a mould, take it out, dry it, nick it all over to make it aerodynamic, give it a coat of paint, pat it on its backside and send it off to market.

Figuratively speaking, but only just, golf balls in the old days were worth their weight in gold. Between 1711 and 1716 the three sons of a certain John Mackenzie were at St Andrews University and so concerned was their father about their tendency to eat into the family fortune that he asked their tutor, James Morice, to keep an eye on expenses. From Morice's accounts, a good-quality featherie golf ball cost 2 shillings. Wooden clubs cost 12 shillings.[139] Hence you could buy a wood for the price of half a dozen good golf balls. At today's prices, if we assume that a half-way decent wood costs £200 (at least), a good golf ball would set you back £32.* Can you imagine what it would be like having to drive off with a £32 golf ball? You would be a gibbering wreck. The lake on the left would grow to the size of the Atlantic, the swamp on the right would take on Jurassic proportions and the fairway down the middle would shrink to the width of a snake's tongue. There are one or two people I could name who would be down £320 before they reached the ninth. This ratio of 6:1, wood to ball, continued more or less constant for 200 years. By 1905, it had fallen to 3:1 in part because the Haskell ball was still relatively new and therefore expensive at 2 shillings.† In that year, you could buy a Forgan driver, cleek or other iron for 6 shillings. (A brassie, presumably because of its brass sole plate, cost 6s 6d.) Now, walk down to your local golf emporium and ask yourself these two questions. Why are drivers so expensive? Do you smell profiteering? If the old ratio of 6:1 applied today, a driver should cost about £9.00. A new Calloway will set you back £300. I leave you, ladies and gentlemen of the poor, benighted and much put upon golfing public, to chew on this.

For as long as the manufacture of balls and clubs was a craft industry, St Andrews and the local economy prospered. The featherie

* Using a ratio of 12: 2 or 6:1

† The gutta ball had sold in 1887 for about 8d (two thirds of a shilling).

was the ideal product for the entrepreneurial St Andreans of the day. It was made by soaking three pieces of cowshide, sewing them together, turning the thing inside out and then stuffing unspecified amounts* of boiled feathers into a small hole left in the top. As it dried, the leather contracted and the feathers expanded, leaving a ball that hopefully was hard and round. What it wasn't was hard wearing. It was easy to cut and the seams tended to open up when wet – which made it an expensive product with a short life span or, in other words, the kind of thing that every struggling caddie with a spare moment dreams of manufacturing. The featherie was wiped out by the gutta ball which could be made by nothing much more complicated than boiling and moulding a rubbery tree sap. The gutta in turn gave way to the wound rubber ball commercialised by Cornell Haskell in 1898.† When automatic ball winding came along two years later, the age of mechanisation had arrived and manufacture was beyond the reach of the small scale St Andrean operations.

The new ball was simply better and there was no going back. A member of the R&A was sufficiently moved by the Haskell to write to *The Times*: 'It must have been in the Spring of 1902 that my brother who was at the time living in Chicago sent me one of the new balls . . . I took it out on to the verandah at the R&A . . . I bounced it onto the concrete floor. It flew up to the roof, much to the surprise of the members sitting there.'[140] Sandy Herd, a St Andrean, paid eight times over the odds to acquire one before the 1902 Open,[141] and ended up beating Vardon and Braid by one shot. Clubs went much the same way as balls, although mass production took a little longer to take hold. Drop-forging techniques

---

* Feathers were measured by the hat-full, but none of the various accounts agrees on how many were needed. Like cooking a stroganoff. If Delia Smith says two tablespoons of Hungarian paprika, Keith Floyd will advise six.

† In a depressing footnote, I should add that the wound rubber ball had actually been invented in St Andrews thirty years earlier by one Duncan Stewart, but he didn't patent it or persevere. If he had, St Andrews might still have a golf ball industry but then, why weep. The history of British invention is littered with discoveries, from the computer down, that have been made here but commercialised in the United States. One more that got away is only another in the middle of a very long list.

for making iron heads were in use early in the 20th century and steel shafts were declared legal (for golfing purposes) in 1929. Thereafter mass-produced balanced sets became possible. Who needs a craftsman to spend hours whittling on a hickory shaft, when you can press a switch and have machines turn out balanced and identical sets in their thousands? Forgans sold out in the 1960s, and that was the end of serious golf club manufacture in St Andrews.

I should mention that The Links road itself, which these days we rather take for granted, owes its very existence to the last pitched battle ever fought in St Andrews.[142] In 1880, the houses on Pilmour Links backed directly onto the golf course and, with everyone going in and out and driving coaches up and down, to step out of the house was to step into a quagmire. The householders wanted a road and the Town Council agreed. Theirs however was not the only view. 'If a road could be built across the Links every time anyone felt like it', some asked, 'where would it all end?' Where indeed. The matter went to the courts, the Council proceeded to build the road, and their opponents in the form of hired gangs of navvies, replied by removing the bottoming and road metal as fast as it was laid. The sight of two gangs of workmen making and unmaking a road was too good to miss and the town took the day off to watch. The Road Committee scratched its collective head and came up with: 'Bribery'. The opposition navvies were offered £1 a day – more than a man would normally earn in a week – to change sides, and change sides they did. They stopped un-laying the road and started laying it. The opposition frantically cast about for replacements, finally dispatching a messenger to Strathkiness (four miles away) to collect all the men and carts available. The Committee scratched again, and up popped: 'Temptation'. Somewhere between St Andrews and Strathkiness, the messenger was persuaded to take a little more for his health than turned out to be good for him. By the time he arrived at his destination, he was 'oblivious to all earthly things' and unable to deliver his message. A squad of Irish labourers were immediately summoned from Dundee. The Committee, now positively humming with creativity, scratched for a third time and produced: 'False Witness'. A Council agent, posing as one of the opposition, intercepted the squad at Guardbridge and told them that their services were no longer required. In one last and desperate throw, the opposition forces re-grouped and, armed with spades and shovels, went down to the Links to do battle. Soon after hand to hand fighting had begun, the Road Committee delved once more into its kitbag of devious devices and out came: 'Free Booze'. By daybreak the casualties consisted of 53 men 'mortal drunk', and the road was duly completed.

The
Necessities
of Life

CHAPTER 12

Eating

WHEN WE FIRST CAME HERE, eating out was not high on the list of 'great things to do in Scotland'. Come to think of it, I don't believe it was on the list at all. Eating out was something you did if you found yourself unable to eat in – if the oven had blown up or someone had had a go at the gas mains with a JCB. I am not talking here about nipping out for a fish supper, which was, and is, a most effective way of taking in essential nutrients and stomach liner should a subsequent visit to the pub be under contemplation. No, I am talking about the idea of eating out as a pleasurable experience, the idea that the eater and his companions can spend a few hours in a place and have fun. This concept was largely unknown in the St Andrews of the late 1970s.

Most eating out then was done in hotels and I have to say that my early experiences here have scarred me for life as far as hotel dining is concerned. I don't know what the idea of a hotel restaurant conjures up for you, but to me it is a place where you book a table, find that you and your wife are the only people in the place apart from one old gent from Yorkshire, and spend the entire evening making sign language to each other so as not to puncture the silence that hangs over you like a bowl of lukewarm leek and potato. After about five minutes of whispered exchanges as to whether it is too late to get up and leave, by which time the soup has arrived and you're stuck, you both become – and you are completely powerless over this – entirely fixated by the eating habits of the other diner. There was one excruciating evening we had in a hotel nearby, when we entered a huge and empty dining room and, no doubt to make things feel cosy, were put at a table next to a fellow who managed to accompany his every mouthful with a purgatorial sniff so harrowing that it sounded as if he was ingesting his food through the wrong organ. We were transfixed.

There have been some nightmare meals served up in Scottish restaurants over the years, and I don't know why this should have been. The raw materials – the meat, the vegetables – are of the finest but something tends to be lost when it reaches the plate. I suspect that part of the problem lies with the great Scottish consumer. He doesn't complain. No matter what muck is put in front of him, he will do his best to force it down. A number of us went to Arran a few years ago and we booked into a place to celebrate an important birthday. One of our party being American, and previously of the opinion that sheep meant wool – 'you mean you eat the little critters' – ordered lamb. Big mistake. The chef – and I use this term only because, in spite of centuries of isolation on these islands from the culinary mainstream, there is no word in the English language for someone who cooks appallingly and is paid to do so – had learnt somewhere that with lamb goes mint sauce. This was a good thought, but one that has to be applied in moderation. Not half a gallon of it worked into every inch of meat and potato, and how, we asked ourselves (mainly to distract poor J.M. who felt obliged, given that someone else was paying, to take a stab at his plateful), did the 'chef' accomplish that curiously light, radioactive green. The rest of us had steak, covered in a mound of sludge with the consistency of mashed peanut, which looked as if it had taken its original form inside the restaurant cat. Did we complain? Well, in a limp sort of way, we might have opined something along the lines of 'Chef doesn't seem quite at his best this evening', but we didn't kick up the sort of right royal stink that, for the sake of every other diner in Scotland, we should have done, and that every self-respecting American would have done.

The staple diet of Scotland used to be porridge (rolled oats), fish and whisky, which was nutritious, filling and conducive to a good night's sleep at the end of a hard day. Today the staple diet is deep fried fish in batter or, as a variant, deep fried batter in batter, followed by sweets or chocolate if you are a child or, for the over 12s, lager. It may not surprise you to learn that Scotland, five or six years ago, was the coronary capital of the globe. More Scots died of coronary heart disease than anywhere in the world, and that is a long list to come bottom of. Today, by dint of extensive propaganda, we have managed to edge ahead of Eastern Europe in the league tables, but we are still worse than England, Western Europe, the United States and every other place that has enough men still standing to keep statistics.

Of course, for the health-conscious tourist, there is always haggis, which can be tasty and is largely without grease – at least I don't think you will be offered it coated in layers of batter and deep fried, but you never know. In the days before BSE, you could probably have tucked into a nice bladder-full without any fear of turning into a gibbering wreck a year or two after putting down your knife and fork but now I am not entirely sure I can recommend it. All those minced unmentionables do seem a bit risky. Having said this, the Japanese Puffer fish (Fugu rubripes) is still widely sought after in Japan, in spite of the fact that 300 Japanese die each year from eating it – so I don't think any lingering BSE baggage need mean that the haggis cause is entirely lost. As a matter of interest, if a teaspoonful of Fugu testes is mixed with hot saké the result is a most coveted aphrodisiac, so the message for the haggis marketing boys is, 'show a little more imagination'. In the meantime, you might like to try the vegetarian haggis, which I am told has its moments.

The good news is, and let me get this in before you cancel your reservations in favour of a week in Paris, that the food in St Andrews is a great deal better than it was. It still has a way to go, but at least today we have restaurants: places that attempt to put something interesting on your plate and on the whole look reasonably pleased to see you. In the 1970s, the usual greeting from a waitress was a raised eyebrow. This was the traditional way in which she would attempt to establish your gastronomic preferences, but to unseasoned travellers, expecting something along the lines of, 'our special this evening is battered puffer fish', the absence of speech, coupled with ignorance of local custom, was mildly unsettling. Would a word or two eventually fall from her lips? Should you wait? Should you speak? All this has gone now, presumably because waitresses have woken up to the fact, which they certainly hadn't woken up to back then, that there is some tenuous connection between talking to customers and hanging on to their jobs. The service these days is better, the food is better and the variety is better – not wonderful, but better.

The best restaurant in St Andrews over the years, the one to which I would award the Palme d'Or, is The Vine Leaf at 131 South Street, which you will find at the end of an enclosed and gloomy passage off the main street. Should you make it to the entrance, you will be well looked after by Ian Hamilton and his wife Morag, who have been dispensing hospitality through the dark days and as other restaurants have come and gone. The menu is imaginative, the cooking is good and the price is not exorbitant and, when you have a wife and three kids to support, that is a pretty attractive combo. Similar fare is provided by the Dolls House in Church Square, behind the town church and close by the town's public lavatories.* A number of restaurants have attempted to make a go of it on this site, without much luck, but it may be that the Dolls House is here to stay. The fixed price lunch is good value and, when the sun is shining, it is pleasant to eat outside and watch the town stroll by. Also good is the Russell, on the Scores and more or less opposite the Catholic church. The Russell has rooms, but since it operates mainly as a bar and restaurant, I don't think of it as a hotel and hence am able to go there without breaking out in a cold sweat. The boss is Gordon de Vries, who has the comforting physique of a patron who dines regularly at his own establishment, and he is generally there to supervise proceedings. The steaks are good and you can eat in the bar or in the pleasantly intimate dining room.

The major Italian restaurant in town is Ciao Roma in South Street, which has managed to bounce back after a debut which didn't exactly have the audience rapturous in appreciation. On opening night, the service was not so much slow, as stationary. The seven o'clock sitting didn't eat before 11, and midnight had come and gone before the nine o'clock tables sniffed the faintest whiff of nourishment. This did no good for blood sugar levels. The person who copped most of the abuse was a poor student, dressed up as a Roman Centurion, who had been given the

---

* The faint whiff of disinfectant is not unplesant.

unpromising task of taking irate customers into the ale-house next door for a placatory beverage. (Bare legs and a breastplate not being ideal dress for that particular drinking establishment, I should perhaps record that the Centurion's last act before quitting that same evening was to go to the gents, hurl his armour to the ground, and sob.) Things, however, have improved since then. It is now possible to visit the restaurant, and eat: usually before Oxfam has to launch an appeal. In fact, things have become so much better that I am going to award Ciao Roma a rosette for the most improved restaurant in town. The last time I was in, the food was good and there were enough bona-fide Italian waiters to give it that 'Mamma cooka the spaghetti' feel. In fact, I was sufficiently in the mood to be about to allow my five words of Italian an airing: until my wife, sensing what was coming, gave me one of her looks.

We have three Indian restaurants in town but, if anything in life is certain, there won't be three for much longer. Indian restaurants here are rather like cereal farmers in economics textbooks. Those of you who have had the misfortune to have ploughed through these may remember a supply and demand graph in the shape of an 'x'. When the price of wheat is high, farmers turn over their acreage to wheat, too much wheat is grown, and the price of wheat falls. Because the price is low, farmers stop planting wheat, so supply falls and the price goes up, and so on ad infinitum. (This was, of course, before the days of the CAP.*) Anyway, this is how Indian restaurants operate in St Andrews. When there is only one, it is packed, so others think 'I know, I will start an Indian restaurant'. The fact is though that, whilst I and many of our friends are happy to eat curry until it oozes out of our spice-saturated pores, there are not enough customers for three restaurants. Sorry boys, but that's how it is. The oldest of the three restaurants is the Balaka at the west end of Market Street. It regularly makes it into the list of 100 best curry restaurants in Britain and has in Mr Rouf

* CAP stands for Common Agricultural Policy, and is a device for taking huge amounts of money out of the pockets of taxpayers in Germany and Britain and distributing it to farmers in France and the other Mediterranean countries. Under the CAP, the laws of supply and demand are suspended. Farmers sell at a given price irrespective of how much they overproduce.

a proprietor who has his own herb and vegetable garden, and likes to get the details right. The newcomers are Café India in Market Street, and the Jahangir in South Street.

My great dread in a restaurant is 'butter'. It used to be everywhere – the higher the prices, the more butter was ladled on – until olive oil (great discovery) pushed north over Hadrian's Wall and gradually squeezed it out. There are one or two places where butter still clings on like a tub of Raquel Welsh in *One Million Years BC*, but these days you would be unlucky to find yourself 'buttered out' as you were routinely not so long ago. Speaking personally, and this is probably a comment on my own inadequate digestive system, I don't cope well with a meal that is fried in butter, has butter in the potatoes, butter on the vegetables and is covered by a sauce that is 90% you know what. I groan under the extra weight, stagger up to bed exuding gases from every orifice and don't shake it off until about four in the morning. If I was being picky, I would have to say that the Grange, about a mile outside St Andrews, is a bit too generous with the Lurpak, which will probably mean that I will never be allowed up there again – which would be a pity, because the Grange has a cosy and attractive bar with an open fire in winter, and in summer from the front, one of the best views of St Andrews.

If you are looking for a sandwich sort of lunch, then there is the West Port which surprisingly is next to the West Port at the west end of South Street. This is run by Australians,* is liberally sprinkled with students during term time, and lays on the sort of baguette and salad lunch you might find on the Continent. Booming consumption of same has recently encouraged the management to lash out on a complete make-over, and the place now comes with a rather up-market restaurant alongside, of the sort that only used to be found in smarter cities. For something more traditional, most of the pubs do lunch these days and there are a cluster of pub/restaurants on Playfair Terrace at the west end of

* The West Port used to be called the Britannia and be run by two doughty and venerable ladies who, when asked for a pint, would produce two half-pints. It may not surprise you to learn that such sensibilities do not trouble the current antipodean ownership.

North Street as it turns into Golf Place and down to the Old Course itself. I have to admit that I have never eaten in any of these, which is my fault and not theirs, but they run from bar food to full dinners (steak, fish etc) and I am told they are good value, cheerful and filling. Ideal before or after a round of golf. The other possibility is Littlejohns on Market Street, which is an American-style steak and burger joint, and the kind of place that makes the British feel they are in the Mid West, and the Midwesterners sure beyond a shadow of doubt that they are in Britain. An alternative burger bar is Ziggy's in Murray Place, whose main claim to fame is that it once served bison burgers. I don't know what the ecological position is on making burgers from animals that I thought were extinct except for half a dozen mating couples in the Yellowstone National Park, but they went down well with Andrew, and with native Americans who were missing the prairie.

There is no shortage of other eateries in town. Some, like Number 33 and Brambles, I haven't visited for many years and are well thought of. Others, like the Inn Town or Lanes (which used to be called Cardinals, and before that Pepitas) have recently opened, as have Costa Coffee, and the North Point Café. All of them enhance the Town's prandial potential. Likewise some of the pubs, such as the Vic and Ogstens, which I only hear about from my kids and where anyone over the age of 25 feels ready for his senior bus pass. But enough of all this. St Andrews is a small place and part of the pleasure is to wander round and have a snoop here or a pint there. Nothing is off limits.

Oh, as a postscript, don't leave without trying the ice cream. Janetta's in South Street has possibly the finest in the country. Andrew, who is a significant consumer in his own right and whose opinion on these matters has to be respected, has been known to argue the case for San Luca in Musselburgh, but I would plump for Janetta's. Our other emporium, Luvians, owned by the Fusaro Brothers, also has sufficiently close genetic connections to the birthplace of excellent ice cream to be worthy of consideration.

CHAPTER 13

Sleeping

LET ME OWN UP at the outset to the fact that I have never lain between the sheets of a St Andrews hotel. I have been admitted through the front door of several, but have never made it upstairs. What mysteries lie beyond, as the visitor ascends, only he or she will know. I did once play golf in Ohio when the course happened to be running a 'promotion'. Whoever hit his ball closest to the flag on the par three 9th would win an all-expenses paid trip to St Andrews, Scotland. For some reason, this really pumped me up. 'The winner of the trip to St Andrews is Michael Tobert from, um, (pause), St Andrews. Gee, Wilbur, can this be right?' And, let's face it, the only way I am going to spend a night in St Andrews is to win one. I am far too mean to part with good money for a hotel here, when I have a perfectly serviceable bed of my own. Accordingly, I walked onto the tee, took immense trouble over my four iron and, with an inevitability that would have broken lesser men years ago, thinned it. It bounced twice on the water surrounding the green, and disappeared.

The most expensive room in St Andrews is to be found at the Old Course Hotel. The Royal Suite will (as I write) set you back £575, but the price includes an oak dining table, a chandelier and an open fire. The lady on the desk who fielded my enquiry was at pains to assure me that this also included breakfast, which I must say, at £575, I had rather taken for granted. If you buy a Rolls-Royce, you don't really expect the salesman to labour the point that the price includes wheels. If you don't fancy the Royal suite, you can pay a couple of hundred pounds less and have a room overlooking the 17th hole, or you can slum it at the back for a trifling £270. If this hasn't put you off, you won't be ruffled by the price of a gin and tonic at the bar. Just don't expect to find too many locals drinking alongside. In the 1970s and 1980s, the hotel had developed two very good techniques for discouraging local custom: the heat and the food. I don't know who used to be in charge of heating, a homesick Saharan perhaps, but the temperature was routinely kept at a level that would kick-start tropical orchids, melt credit cards and roast any natives who had the temerity to wander in without prior acclimatisation. As for the food, I did once have lunch there. A huge plate arrived on which next to nothing was visible. A tiny anthill of pasta that I downed in two gulps, with a further gulp when I saw the bill. Things are better now. The managers have wrested back control of the boiler for one thing, and my impression, from limited exposure, is that Japanese ownership has raised standards considerably. It is a five-star hotel after all. What I would say, and I say this from the certainty of regular usage, is that its Health Spa is excellent, with staff who could not be more helpful.

Next in line, with rather better views across the 18th and along the West Sands, is the four-star, Rusacks Marine Hotel. To enjoy the view from your hotel bedroom, be prepared to fork out similar sorts of amounts as at the Old Course Hotel. The building itself is ideally situated halfway along the 18th, and has a certain Victorian grandness about it – except that, somehow, it manages to give the impression that its best days are behind it, which I suppose they are. It was built in 1887 by Johann Wilhelm Christ of Rusack, formerly of Bad Harzburg in Lower Saxony, to cater for well-heeled Victorian tourists who had just started to discover the delights of St Andrews[143], and it quickly became a favourite watering hole for Royalty downwards. If you begin life this well, you are almost bound to slip a little as the years progress, and it has. The last time I went in to Rusacks was for a Canadian wedding reception, and a magnificent 'do' it was too. All the Canadians wore kilts, the piper was Canadian and, as the procession left the church, the American and Japanese tourists lining the streets happily took photographs in the fond belief that they were watching a real Scottish wedding. Which in a sense they were and, in the sense that they were not, who was I to tell them otherwise.

The three-star hotels are Rufflets, the Scores and St Andrews Golf Hotel. Rufflets is excellent, has its own gardens, but is out of town. The others are sited on the Scores so that whatever else, you can wake up to that wonderful sound of seagulls wheeling and screeching overhead. When consciousness first returns and you find yourself in a strange room but can't quite piece together where the hell you actually are, these are the sounds that say, 'Hey, I am at the seaside'. Great sounds they are too, but not confined to the hotels. The bed-and-breakfasts provide gull music, too. If what you want is some clean sheets on which to rest your head at night, and a thumping good breakfast in the morning, the B&Bs are the answer. I could make one or two suggestions both good and bad but, bearing in mind that this is a small town and that I hope to carry on walking for a few more years yet, let me encourage you to contact the Tourist Information Office in Market Street. They produce a brochure listing all available accommodation, so ring them up and ask them to send you a copy.* You may be staggered to discover that you will pay nothing for this service even if you live in Outer Mongolia.

* Bear in mind, when reading the brochure, that the Scottish Tourist Board is more generous when it comes to awarding stars than the AA.

CHAPTER 14

Booking a Tee Time

'Look, you pick up the phone, speak to the pro's shop and book a time. Either that or you find a member and play with him. Right?' Wrong. First of all, whilst we do have phones, there is no pro. There are plenty of pros who will be more than happy to give you a lesson, but none who are attached to the Links.* There are no members. There are plenty of golf clubs – the R&A, the New Club, The St Andrews Club, St Rule, St Regulus and others – but none of these owns the St Andrews golf courses. Allow me to explain.

The Links land of St Andrews had been granted to the burgh in 1123 by the King, David 1, and has, with occasional interruptions†, remained town land ever since. Now town land, these days, is legally deemed to be owned by the local authority which, by virtue of a series of misguided administrative changes, is no longer an amalgam of public-spirited St Andreans, but the huge and distant Fife Council.** It is Fife Council that owns the Links:

---

* The definition of Links Land is sandy ground near the seashore, covered with turf or coarse grass, and either level or gently undulating. In other words, the ideal spot for a golf course.

† For most of the 19th century the Links were in private hands (for a while as a commercial rabbit farm), a state of affairs brought about by the parlous condition of the town's finances. The Town Council decided to privatise the Links partly to raise cash and partly to finance its drinking habit. It is not clear whether the cash shortages caused the drinking or vice versa but, according to the historian David Hay Fleming, the Council found it impossible 'to discuss even trivial municipal matters without the aid of wine and punch, and greater matters were celebrated with an abundance of strong liquor'. Fortunately, thanks to the good offices of a local family, the Cheapes, and to the R&A, the consequences of this over-indulgence were not as disastrous as they might have been. The Links were returned to town ownership.

** If you were to allow me one political point, it would be that St Andrews is disenfranchised. It elects four out of the seventy-eight seats on Fife Council. The other seventy-four come mainly from the bigger Fife towns of Kirkcaldy, Glenrothes, Dunfermline, Leven and Cowdenbeath, places which, delightful though they may be, have as much sympathy for St Andrews as chalk has for cheese. The sooner the new Scottish Parliament comes to realise that a country the size of Scotland does not need both a Parliament and regional government covering swathes of country as large as Fife, the safer St Andrews and its Links will be. A Scottish Parliament at the top and a Town Council at local level is all we need.

which would be as much an unmitigated disaster as entrusting a beautiful young virgin to the tender mercies of Jack the Ripper, were it not for the fact that the management of the Links is, by Act of Parliament, in the hands of the Links Trust*. Hallelujah, and long may it so remain.

The duty of the Links Trust is to maintain the Links *'as a public park and place of public resort and recreation for the residents of the town of St Andrews and others resorting thereto'*. Recreation means golf. It doesn't have to. It could mean football (which has an ancient tradition on the Links), but whilst I would never underestimate the sort of strange things that can happen to sensible men when they sit down together in a committee, I would be truly astonished to pick up the *St Andrews Citizen* (the town weekly) one morning and find that the Old Course was to be relaid as football pitches. This would expose the inadequacy of current aphorisms such as barking mad, out to lunch and one wedge short of the full set. A new terminology expressing the ultra-lunatic, lunacy beyond the scope of imagination, would have to be invented. And yet, no sooner do we state that certain outer limits are unreachable, what happens? The old boundary is challenged. Listen to this. It is from Fife Council's 1998 'Consultation Paper on the Future of the St Andrews Links Trust'. We are asked to consider the following question: 'Should St Andrews Links continue to be dedicated for the use and enjoyment by the public and the playing of golf?' OK, ignoring the sentence's grammatical idiosyncrasies, here is a counter question? Are they serious? Do they contemplate for one nanosecond that the Links might not be dedicated to the playing of golf? No. It cannot be. Not even from Fife Council. It must be an academic exercise, one of those questions expecting the answer 'yes'. Anything else might just tip me over the edge.

Anyway, for the time being at least, bookings are handled by the Links Trust. You can ring them up for a time on the Old Course but, if you want to play in the summer, ring early. A year ahead is good. If you can't think that far ahead, you can book a

---

* Whilst the Council is highly influential in the Links Trust, with 3/8 of the vote, it does not, thank heavens, have a majority.

time through the Keith Prowse agency who, controversially, bought a block of tee times from the Trust some years ago. It isn't cheap. A round on the Old, a round on the New and two nights at the Old Course Hotel will set you back £1,200 (and by the time you read this, the price will almost certainly be higher). Alternatively, you can put your name in the ballot the day before you wish to play and, if your name comes out of the hat, a round on the Old Course will cost about £75'.* From time to time, people mutter that the ballot has been rigged, or the starter bribed, but frankly, and call me naïve, I don't believe it. I have never known anyone who has bribed the starter and never seen anyone try. However desperate you are to play, I wouldn't recommend it. I can imagine the look that would appear on the starter's face and I wouldn't wish to be opposite it when it does. A quiet word is easier in private clubs. I have been taken round North America when my guide and mentor would begin the day by arming himself with bags of donuts which he would then distribute liberally, along with some engaging chat, in lieu of green fees – but the North Americans are generous people and, because the courses are owned by the members, able to use discretion. Here, the courses are owned by the community and trying to talk the starter into squeezing you onto the start sheet is a little like trying to persuade a traffic warden, who has already licked the end of his pen, not to write out a parking ticket. However, if you are prepared to put in the hours, you can usually find a game. Go down to the starters box early and hang around. There will be two or three-balls going out, or someone will scratch.

If you can't get a time on the Old, or it is Sunday when the Old is always closed, you can always try the New, Jubilee, Eden, Strathtyrum or Balgove, which are listed in order of difficulty (although many would say that the Jubilee is more testing than the Old). The New is a great course, particularly if you can't move the ball from left to right. The Jubilee is long, and punishing if you stray from the straight and narrow. The Eden has recently

* Locals I'm pleased to say, pay much less if they buy a season ticket, but then many of them can remember the not-to-distant days when their golf was free.

been turned into a full-sized golf course which makes it a tougher proposition but not necessarily better. It's less natural now and quite what a lake thinks it is doing on the 14th and 15th holes in the middle of sandy links land is beyond me. The Strathtyrum is for family golf and the Balgove for beginners.

Sundries

CHAPTER 15

The Weather

NO ACCOUNT OF ST ANDREWS would be complete without a brief word on those many and varied occurrences that come at you from the heavens above. This is a subject that most commentators prefer to gloss over. Were you to glance at any of the photo-rich coffee-table books on St Andrews, you would be stunned by a vista of sun-drenched fairways and sweltering students. A veritable Riviera, you might conclude, with green grass. Do not be fooled. Patient men took the photographs. There is a very good reason why the grass is green. It is called rain: which occurs in January, March, April, May, June, July, August and December. For some reason, probably to do with the avoidance of mass suicide, February and November are generally dry and sunny. This is not to say that it always rains in the other months. It doesn't. Sometimes it hails, sometimes it snows, blows a gale, or is merely windy in a gusty, is it an 8-iron or a wedge, kind of way. Sometimes it pours for 10 minutes, then the sun comes out, and just when you have struggled free of your waterproof trousers, it pours again. Sometimes, there is high pressure across the rest of the country, whilst St Andrews shivers under a *haar*.* And sometimes, let it be said, the weather is gloriously, blissfully hot; at which time the Auld Toun is the finest place on earth and any thought of shelling out hard-earned coin of the realm for a holiday abroad seems daft. In any event, the weather here, whatever its peccadilloes, is not boring, and there is enough of it to keep the unsuspecting on their toes.

---

* A *haar* is a sea-fret or mist that rolls in from the sea. It can be T-shirt weather in Cupar, and two sweaters in St. Andrews.

CHAPTER 16

Dates for the Diary

ST ANDREWS HAS A NUMBER of recurring events each year which visitors may wish to note. Put a mark by April (the second week usually) not in anticipation of climatic leniency (see above) but because of the Kate Kennedy procession. This is the moment when students, in period costume, process around the town impersonating major players in the town's history. Kate Kennedy, the central figure in the parade, was either the niece of Bishop James Kennedy who founded the University's St Salvator's College in 1450 or, more inspiringly, a version of the unpronounceable Gaelic Cath Cinnaechaidh, meaning the birth of spring. The uninitiated may find Kate in need of a shave, but this is because the Kate Kennedy Club, which organises the event, is men-only. This may explain why some students regard the Club as elitist, sexist and incurably public school. Others – no doubt those who are elitist, sexist and incurably public school – see it as a fine old institution that does a great deal of good work, and puts on the best student ball of the year. Irrespective, the parade is a charming spectacle and a fine way for the town to doff its cap to its illustrious forbears.

May Day is not really a major event in the town calendar, but it deserves to be recorded: as a testimony to pluck. 1 May is the beginning of summer, officially (not, of course, barometrically) and, in times gone by, was when the ancient Celts indulged in a rollicking good fire festival. In celebration of such flickering memories, St Andrews students plunge at dawn into a glacial North Sea,* to the strains of the University glee club singing unaccompanied six-part harmony. Yes, folks, the students actually wake up (not an everyday occurrence), go down to the sea, peel off their waterproofs, sweaters, shirts, vests and whatever else, put on

---

* What kind of fire festival is this, you may wonder. Me too.

A Selection of St Andrews Alumni from the Kate Kennedy Parade
From the 15th century comes Laurence of Lindores, the Scottish theologian, the sinister 'Inquisitor of Heretical Pravity', and the man who put a match to the first bonfire of a Protestant martyr in Scotland. From the 16th century, John Napier of Merchiston, the leading mathematician of his day, who invented logarithms, as well as sundry instruments of war, such as a mirror which used the power of the sun to burn enemy ships – presumably not for the home market. The 17th century produced James Graham, Marquis of Montrose, the brilliant Civil War general, who celebrated winning the student archery contest, the Silver Arrow, by shooting an arrow over St Salvator's tower and into the hat (being worn at the time) of the Dean of the Faculty of Arts. The 18th century gave us Robert Fergusson, the poet who inspired Burns and who died at the age of 24, in the Edinburgh Bedlam, of drink and debauchery. And from the 19th comes Elizabeth Garret Anderson, the first female medical practitioner in Britain, after whom the women's hospital in London is named. And many more. One of the best is James Crichton of Eliock (1560-83) aka the Admirable Crichton, who added a new dimension to the meaning of the word 'precocious'. He entered St Andrews University aged 10, and graduated at 14. He was a fine horseman, swordsman and musician, fluent in 8 languages (some say 12), the best debater in Europe and the man who (reputedly) never told a lie. He was murdered in his early twenties. On his way back from a nocturnal assignation with his mistress, he was attacked by a drunken gang. Just when he was about to lay his assailants to waste, he recognised their leader, Vicenzo, the son of his patron the Duke of Mantua. Laying down his sword, he allowed himself to be killed. (Either that or Vicenzo, alarmed at Crichton's influence at court, stabbed him in the dark.) J.M.Barrie, creator of Peter Pan and Rector of St Andrews University, wrote a play called *The Admirable Crichton* and, in case you are thinking of reading it, you may wish to know that it has nothing to do with James Crichton.

swimming costumes and dive in, probably breaking the ice as they do so, whilst other students, music in hand, sing. Should you happen to stumble across this scene unexpectedly, be warned: it can be disorientating – in much the same way as stumbling through a time warp and finding yourself surrounded by escaped lunatics can be disorientating.

The Lammas Fair comes to town in the first week of August.

Keep away unless under 18. The Lammas is venerable, which is the best I can say about it. In the Middle Ages, there used to be five annual market fairs. The first and the largest was the Senzie (or Synod) fair which was held after Easter in the Cathedral grounds, and coincided with the gathering in town of all the clergy from the Archbishop down. The other fairs were in June, August, September and November, but today the only one that remains is the Lammas or Loaf Mass market, which was originally a hiring fair for agricultural workers. By the turn of this century, the Lammas was attracting freshly scrubbed young men and women, a town band, and a gentle horse carousel outside Jimmy MacGregor's emporium in Market Street. Today, it occupies most of South Street and Market Street, predominantly consists of rides with names like 'Terminator', 'Gladiator' and 'Kamikaze', is grotesquely overpriced, deafening and completely devoid of charm. However, the kids love it, and we have had to be pretty devious in the past to contrive to be out of town at just the right weekend.

September (the first three weeks) is the Autumn Meeting of the R&A. Overseas members flood in, and the uniform (blue blazer, grey flannel trousers, vermilion visage, club tie) is everywhere to be seen. If you are coming to play golf, make sure you have your start times confirmed before you set out. Opportunities for visitors on the Old and the New courses are in short supply. One of the traditions of the Meeting is that, on the last day, the Captain-elect plays himself into office. The honorary professional of the Club (currently John Panton) tees up his ball, the Club's 1892 cannon* fires and the Captain drives off. The caddie who collects his ball is awarded a gold sovereign so, consequently, the caddies arrange themselves down the fairway at positions that each feels will give himself the best chance in the resulting stramash. When the Duke of Windsor drove himself in, in 1922, the caddies were described as standing 'disloyally close'.

October sees the Dunhill World matchplay / strokeplay champi-

---

* The Club's first cannon had been bought from a Prussian captain in 1837 for £2. Because of worries about danger to shipping in St. Andrews Bay, it was replaced in 1892 by a more expensive version.

onship. Its format is curious to say the least, and I won't bore you with the details. As a dramatic event, it rates 1 on the nail-biting scale (10 is chewed down to the quick), with the result that the crowds are about as thick on the ground as a mid-morning bus queue. This means that you can stroll out to the links and stand within a few feet of the world's best, without having to use your elbows. John Daly and Tiger Woods might require a slight nudge to get yourself to the very front but, as for the rest, you can wander unimpeded. The Chinese team will probably be glad of your company. Once every five years or so, the major golfing event in town is not the Dunhill, but the Open (or, as the Americans prefer to call it, the British Open). If the weather is half-way reasonable, St Andrews in the third week of July in an Open year is the place to be. The pavements heave with chattering enthusiasts, restaurants luxuriate in that sublime moment when they can turn people away, and it's party time.

The middle of November is Raisin Weekend, which for students in the town is one of the major events of the year, and for the rest of us is when we thank God that we no longer have to go through all that again. Raisin Weekend harks back to the earliest days of the University and was probably some sort of Rite of Passage into academic life. Today, when a 1st year student, known in the university tongue as a bejant(ine) or fresher, arrives at the university he or she is adopted by her academic parents who are either tertians (3rd year) or magistrands (4th year). On Raisin Sunday, the fresher goes to tea with his or her academic 'mother' (vodka jelly is a favourite, apparently) before being picked up by 'Dad' and introduced to the after-hours nooks and crannies of student life. In return, the student provides a bottle of wine, which is deemed to be today's equivalent of a pound of raisins.* Hence the name 'Raisin' Weekend. On Monday, freshers go to their mums who dress them up in a costume which, bearing in mind this is November, always seems a little skimpy, and Dad then presents them with a Raisin receipt in Latin and a present which they then have to carry around. This is nor-

---

* It is probably immaterial to point out that today's equivalent of a pound of raisins is a pound of raisins.

mally either large, such as a broken bathtub, or obscene. The pleas-
antries draw to a close with a gathering in the Big Quad at 11am
where Freshers are supposed to sing the first verse of the Gaudie in
Latin. The Gaudie is 'Gaudeamus igitur, iuvenes dum sumus', meaning 'we are only young once so if we are going to have some fun,
now is the time'. According to the alternative student prospectus,
'Onion', what actually happens is that the Freshers pelt each other
with shaving foam and assorted noxious substances. At 12 o'clock,
the clock strikes and all go home to wake up 24 hours later swearing that they have forever touched their last drop. The University
looks on all this from a great height, but does provide a help line
throughout Sunday night and into the early hours of Monday, in
case a local resident stumbles across something he feels he should
report: such as a student who has palpably eaten too many raisins.

The year winds down in December with an increase in traditional pastimes like Scottish country dancing and alcoholic consumption, all of which culminates in Hogmanay (Old Year's
Night). Highland dancing is one of those things that indelibly
marks out the interloper so, should you arrive at this time of year,
a few tips, distilled from my twenty years experience of causing
mayhem on the dance floor, might be in order. First, dress. This
can cause the uninitiated some anxiety but the one thing to
remember is, don't wear a kilt unless you know what you are
doing. It implies proficiency. If you find yourself confronted by a
rental salesman who won't take no for an answer, at least resist the
little ballet shoes. Some people do wear them, but I never think
they look quite right on a sixteen-stone Scotsman with hairy legs.
Tartan trews and a decent pair of stout shoes will do you much
better. Second, the steps. What you have to remember is that
although a dance may look completely random, it is in fact made
up of a few basic patterns such as: holding hands and dancing
round in a circle; hopping from foot to foot while facing your
partner or someone else's (known as setting); a figure of eight; dis-
appearing behind the back of the fellow standing next to you
(casting off); twirling your partner round and round (birling); and
making a teapot shape by putting one hand forward in the shape
of a spout and, optionally, making a handle by putting the other

hand on hip – but definitely not recommended if you couldn't say no to the ballet shoes. Third, the dances. The difficulty with the dances is not the steps, but the order in which they appear. What immediately informs the initiated is the name. 'Ah, yes, we're dancing the Duke of Perth's Second Mistress, that's circle, right hand teapot, set, figure of eight, left hand teapot, set, cast off. Got it?' If, like me, such obscure appellations do not immediately trigger the above recitation, you need to pay particular attention to my fourth and final tip, choosing a partner. This is vital. Gentlemen, don't make the mistake of dancing with a girl just because she's pretty. Big and bossy is what you need. Ladies, I would choose the fellow in the ballet shoes.

Christmas is something of a side-show in Scotland. It wasn't all that long ago that it was a working day, no doubt on the principle that 'the better the day, the better the deed'. The main event is Hogmanay. The morning of 1 January bears witness to the night before. The only people stirring are those staggering home from someone else's party, holding their heads on with one hand and groping for direction with the other. Otherwise, nothing moves until lunchtime. The old year ends with a blowout, and the new one begins with the mother of all headaches.

CHAPTER 17

Visitors

BY AND LARGE, and taking the rough with the smooth, St Andrews enjoys its visitors. I would go as far as to say that it finds them stimulating. Money is involved, of course, but it's more than that. If you live in a place that is nine-tenths of the way to the Arctic Circle, it is immensely flattering when the rest of the world chooses to beat a path to your door. OK, there is nowhere to park, and the traffic in South Street can move a little sluggishly but, though we might moan from time to time, in our heart of hearts we regard it as a small price to pay. Not all tourist places can say the same. Ever been to a French ski resort? Or Paris? If the locals there like their visitors, they have a very funny way of showing it. And, if you don't want to be treated like something the cat's brought in, you must speak French. Simply making an effort, which is usually good enough in most countries, is not sufficient. In France, you have to know subjunctives. Here in St Andrews, we don't mind if you don't speak English. It's just that we won't understand any-thing you say.

Getting here is not always straightforward. If you come by plane, you can find yourself at Edinburgh Airport, where it ought to be easy to hop onto a train to St Andrews. The railway line goes right past the airport, after all. The problem is that there is no way of getting from the terminal to the nearest station, South Gyle, and, even if there were, the trains to St Andrews don't stop there. I wish I could offer some simple explanation for this but I am afraid that, beyond uttering the words ScotRail (or should that be Railtrack?) and glancing imploringly heavenward, I can't. What you have to do is to go into Edinburgh, catch a train from Waverley Station or Haymarket, and as you pass through South Gyle Station on the way north an hour and a half later, you may wish to reflect on the mysteries of life.

If you are travelling by day, the guard will normally make an announcement when the train is approaching Leuchars. This is where you should get off. If you have come on the London sleeper, nobody will announce anything. This, presumably, is because the guard has the crazed idea that after the driver has shunted, decelerated, accelerated, stopped stone dead and done everything in his power for the last six hours to catapult his charges out of their bunks and into the handbasin, some passengers might still be sleeping. So here is a tip. If you are coming from the south, the platform will be on your right. This is more important than you may think. If you are looking out of the window on the left side, and gazing sleepily into a field as the train slides to a halt, there is absolutely nothing to intimate that you are in a station. And you don't want to have to catch the next train back from Dundee. Oh, and the other thing is, if you have more suitcases and golf clubs than you can carry, make sure you are first off the train. Don't let any little old ladies stand in your way. There are only two luggage trolleys on the platform.

Considering everything, it is amazing how many people manage to hack their way through. But come they do, in just about all shapes, sizes, denominations, genders and declensions, and from just about everywhere. Americans, Japanese, Italians, Australians, you name it. We even have Finns here, which is quite a laugh. Anybody who hasn't heard Finnish, should re-route immediately to Helsinki. It's so hilariously improbable. No European language should be allowed to sound like that. You can get a fix on it by thinking of a cavalry platoon trotting over cobblestones or somebody with extremely badly fitted dentures caught in a fit of unstoppable teeth chattering. Our stock in trade though is Americans, who have a laudable fascination with where things started. Quite a few end up staying on. In 1998, we had at least two pairs of Alaskans, though quite why I never discovered. They might have been waiting to put on fat in preparation for the journey home or, if their idea of a sultry summer's evening was acquired in Anchorage, could it be that they found St Andrews hot? Anyway, the great thing about all these visitors descending on us is the money it saves. Who needs to fork out for foreign travel when you can stay home and see the world.

The town, in a slightly amateurish kind of way, does its best to lay on entertainment for its visitors. During the summer, various performers and troupes, usually of the mild and musical variety, appear intermittently outside the town church, and occasionally the entertainment committee slips a gear and puts on something bizarre, like an ostrich. This ostrich was on parade in Logies Lane, but to our considerable regret it didn't take the opportunity to run amok down South Street. There is also entertainment provided by private enterprise, otherwise known as busking. The pipers take the sea beat by the Bow Butts, but less deafening instruments work closer in on selected pitches in Market Street and South Street. They make £20 an hour, I'm told, but can I persuade Anna, my eldest, to take out her saxophone? I cannot.

Postscript

CHAPTER 18

St Andrews in 2020

IF EVER A CITY'S FUTURE was contained in its past, it's St Andrews. Just take out the long lens and look at the last thousand years. Pilgrims have come (for 500 years), pilgrims have gone (400 years), and pilgrims have returned (100 years), only this time it is not a cross they clutch lovingly to their chest, but the latest titanium-enriched, tungsten-plated knobstick. But that's a detail. The golfers arriving in droves come to worship and, by the way, are the kind of pilgrims that tourist agencies would die for: immaculately behaved, respectfully awe-struck and, more to the point, rich. Not a pot-bellied lager lout in sight. Another couple of hundred years of the like, and the roller coaster will have a lovely symmetrical look to it. And why not? Since there isn't a statistician in the world who will tell you that golf is about to become less popular, what can the future hold but more golfers and more prosperity?

Which is all very alluring, and may well be right, except that complacency has a nasty habit of coming to a sticky end. Plenty of things might come along to upset the apple-cart. What about natural disasters? I am not thinking here about earthquakes (this is St Andrews not San Andreas), hurricanes (hardly happen), drought (I wish), or pestilence (whose days are thankfully over unless a new strain of super bug with a predilection for golfers emerges). No, what worries me is the potentially catastrophic consequence of a shift in the Gulf Stream, or North Atlantic Drift as it is more properly called. Not enough people pay attention to the Gulf Stream; 99% of St Andrews couldn't care less about it. Yet there it is, meandering across the North Atlantic like a liquid dagger pointed at our very heart. The problem is global warming and the melting of the arctic ice cap. There are icebergs the size of the Isle of Man heading south at this very moment, to say nothing of those sheets of cracked ice chunking out of the North Pole. I can see them now making straight for the poor old Gulf Stream, diving in and lying lazily on their backs as the tropical waters waft them in our direction. Apparently, the response of the North Atlantic Drift to imminent refrigeration is to change course. It's starting to turn right instead of going straight on – which means that the palm trees that line the main street of Plockton* may soon be a thing of the past. The plain fact is that, should the warm waters of the Gulf Stream desert us, Scotland will acquire a climate not unlike Newfoundland. Nothing wrong with Newfoundland, you understand, particularly if you like snow, but it might not be everybody's ideal location for a golfing holiday.

The developers don't believe any of this, of course. If they did, they wouldn't be buying up land and adding blots to the landscape as fast as they can seduce the Council's planning committee. Neither do my kids. I asked them to spend five minutes (I know my limitations) on brainstorming the way St Andrews will look in 2020. Let the wacky ideas flow, I told them. The initial flurry was big on things American – Pizza Hut, McDonalds, a multiplex cinema complex and car park, and Disneyworld. The next wave, by which time they were warming to the task, toyed with high-rise flats, spaghetti junction (where the North Haugh is now) and Leuchars Airforce Base converted into a major Scottish airport. Changing tack, they then opined that the goo 'flowing' through the Kiness Burn would be found to contain a cure for cancer. At this point, I glowed with pride and left them in peace to debate whether clubbing facilities and the old Cathedral could march hand-in-hand into the next millennium.

They might be right, who knows, but I have a feeling that St Andrews will not surrender its traditional values without a struggle. My guess is that, in twenty years time, we will still be queuing patiently in the Post Office for the privilege of buying a stamp, the traffic wardens will still be patrolling the streets with the same endearing mix of good humour and tolerance, and the only new development may be a tasteful hologram of the Chairman of Fife Council modestly displayed on the exterior wall of the R&A.

---

*Plockton is on the west coast of Scotland, where the Gulf Stream gets its first taste of dry land.

Paradise will still be paradise and, if the Scot Nats don't kick me out, come 2020, I'll be here hacking divots out of the hallowed turf. That is, of course, if 'ah'm still tae the fore'.

Useful Addresses

British Golf Museum
(The history of golf and its personalities from then to now)
Bruce Embankment, St Andrews, Fife KY16 9AB
Tel: +44 1334 478880. Fax: +44 1334 473306
Website: *www.britishgolfmuseum.co.uk*

The Byre Theatre
(New £5.3m theatre being built with lottery money)
36 South Street, St Andrews, Fife KY16 9JT
Tel: +44 1334 476288. Fax: +44 1334 475370
e-mail: byretheatre@btinternet.com

Jurek Pütter
(Wonderfully researched re-creations of medieval St Andrews)
25 Tom Morris Drive, St Andrews, Fife KY16 8EW
e-mail: jurek@jurekputter.freeserve.co.uk
Tel: +44 1334 470197
Website: *www.jurekputter.freeserve.co.uk*

St Andrews Links Trust
(For booking tee times and answering golf-related questions)
Pilmour House, St Andrews, Fife KY16 9SF
Information: Tel: +44 1334 66666. Fax: +44 1334 466664
                   e-mail: linkstrust@standrews.org.uk
                   Website: *www.standrews.org.uk*
Reservations: Fax: +44 1334 477036
                   Website: *www.linksnet.co.uk*

St Andrews Museum
(Tells the St Andrews story down the ages)
Kinburn Park, Double Dykes Road, St Andrews, Fife KY16 9DP
Tel: +44 1334 412690. Fax: +44 1334 412691

St Andrews Preservation Trust Museum
(Good collection of old St Andrews photos and various exhibitions)
12 North Street, St Andrews, Fife KY16 9PW
Tel: +44 1334 477629

Tourist Information Office
(Up-to-date info on where to stay, things to do etc.)
70 Market Street, St Andrews, Fife KY16 9NU
Tel: +44 1334 472021. Fax: +44 1334 478422

The University of St Andrews
(In case you need an excuse to spend four years at the home of golf)
Tel: +44 1334 476161
Website: *www.st-and.ac.uk*

www.saint-andrews.co.uk
(For moving pictures and a potted history of the town as well as links to other web sites)

Tables

Table 1: *Chronology*

Date	Event

Early Days

Date	Event
79	Romans reach River Tay
300	Romans decide they have had enough
350	St Rule lands with bones of St Andrew (approx)
747	Monastery exists in Kilrimont (St Andrews)
970s	Bishop Cellach II goes to Rome for confirmation
1000	St Andrews is HQ of Scottish Church
1070s	Fothad II builds St Rule's Church

12th century

Date	Event
1100	First harbour at St Andrews
1123	Links land granted to Burgh of St Andrews
1130	Alternative date for founding of St Rule's Church (1130-50)
1160	Cathedral founded

13th century

Date	Event
1200	First Castle in place
1270	West end of Cathedral blows down in a gale
1296	English occupy Castle
1297	Wallace defeats English at Stirling Bridge
1298	Edward I defeats Wallace at Falkirk and burns St Andrews

14th century

Date	Event
1301	Scots appeal to Pope Boniface during Wars of Independence against England
1301	Edward I strips lead from Cathedral roof
1314	Robert Bruce defeats Edward II at Bannockburn

1314	Bishop Lamberton recovers Castle from English
1318	Cathedral consecrated
1320	Declaration of Arbroath
1328	Edward III gives up his claim to Scotland and acknowledges Scottish Independence
1329	Death of Bruce
1333	Scots defeated at Halidon Hill
1337	30,000 pilgrims come to St Andrews
1337	Andrew Moray retakes St Andrews Castle from English and levels it
1378	Fire in Cathedral

15th century

1400	Golf played at St Andrews (probably)
1400	Castle rebuilt
1410	University founded
1412	Holy Trinity Church moved to South Street
1414	Papal Bull recognises St Andrews University
1450	St Salvator's College founded
1457	James II bans golf
1472	Bishop Graham made Archbishop
1479	William Dunbar takes degree

16th century

1512	St Leonard's College founded
1513	Defeat of Scots at Flodden
1517	Luther nails his 95 complaints against Rome to his church door in Wittenberg
1528	Burning of Protestant martyr Patrick Hamilton
1529	Plague in St Andrews (not the first or the last)
1533	Burning of Protestant martyr Henry Forrest
1537	St Mary's College founded
1544	Henry VIII sacks Edinburgh
1546	Burning of Protestant martyr George Wishart
1546	Cardinal Beaton murdered. Siege of St Andrews Castle

1552	Archbishop Hamilton confirms town's right to play golf and football on the links
1558	Burning of Protestant martyr Walter Myln
1559	Sack of the Cathedral (John Knox incites mob)
1560	Reformation Parliament ends Catholicism as the established religion of Scotland
1568	First reference to a woman playing golf (Mary Queen of Scots)

17th century

1603	James VI of Scotland becomes first Stewart King of England as James I of England. Remembers to take golf clubs to London
1618	Start of Silver Arrow competition
1645	Scottish Parliament sits at Parliament Hall in St Andrews
1655	Pier collapses
1656	Pier rebuilt with stones from Castle and Cathedral
1660	Restoration of Monarchy after the Protectorate of Cromwell – Charles II on throne
1672	Pett supplies golf clubs to Marquess of Montrose
1679	Murder of Archbishop Sharp
1698	University debates whether to move to Perth

18th century

1707	Act of Union unites England and Scotland
1736	Statutes against witchcraft repealed
1743	Early indications of golf clubs shipped to Charleston, USA
1744	Honourable Company of Edinburgh Golfers founded
1745	Storm wrecks St Andrews fishing fleet
1754	Society of St Andrews Golfers founded
1754	End of Silver Arrow competition
1758	Benjamin Franklin awarded honorary LL.D
1762	James Wilson earns degree
1764	Old Course reduced from 22 holes to 18

1772	St Leonard's buildings sold to Robert Watson
1773	Visit of Dr Samuel Johnson to St Andrews
1773	Roof of St Salvator's Chapel crashes to earth
1776	American Declaration of Independence
1785	Mining rights on Links sold to Charles Beaumont
1785	Lunardi lands his balloon and plays the Old
1797	Links sold to Dempsters for rabbit farm
1798	Rebuilding of Holy Trinity

19th century

1800	John Honey swims five times to wreck of *Janet of Macduff*
1801	Castle's Great Hall falls into sea
1803	Fishing fleet brought from Shetlands
1821	James Cheape acquires Links
1821	Tom Morris born at 121 North Street
1834	William IV gives R&A Royal status
1834	Opening of Madras School
1836	Samuel Messieux hits featherie 360 yards
1848	The gutta-percha ball replaces the featherie
1852	The railway reaches St Andrews
1858	Allan Robertson breaks 80 on the Old
1867	Himalayas, Ladies Putting Club, founded
1868	Haunted tower opened
1875	Death of Young Tom Morris
1876	University numbers decline to 130
1879	Collapse of Tay Bridge
1880	Links Road war
1892	Marquess of Bute becomes Rector
1893	R&A buys Links from Cheapes
1893	Freddie Tait drives 13th green (341 yards)
1894	Freddie Tait sets course record of 72 on the Old
1894	Town Council buys Links from R&A
1894	Links Act lays down rules for management of Links
1898	Introduction of wound rubber Haskell ball

20th century

1900	Death of Freddie Tait in Boer War
1901	Andrew Carnegie becomes Rector
1903	Step Rock Pool built
1907	Reconstruction of Holy Trinity begins
1908	Death of Old Tom Morris
1914	Passenger trips from harbour ended
1929	R&A legalises steel shafts
1933	Craig Wood drives Spectacles (430 yards)
1946	Links Act removes right of locals to free golf
1958	Bobby Jones awarded Freedom of City
1960-99	Golf flourishes, the University expands, the 'government' of St Andrews passes to Kirkcaldy, developers move in and the town awaits the next millennium.

Table 2: The Bishops and Archbishops of St Andrews

Date	Bishop
1028-1055	Maelduin
c.1055	Tuthald
c.1070-1093	Fothad
c.1107-1115	Turgot
1123-1159	Robert
1160-1162	Arnold
1163-1178	Richard
1178-1188	John Scot
1189-1202	Roger
1202-1238	William Malvoisin
1239-1253	David de Bernham
1254	Abel de Golin
1255-1271	Gamelin
1271-1279	William Wishart
1279-1297	William Fraser
1297-1328	William Lamberton
1328-1332	James Ben
1342-1385	William Landallis
1385-1401	Walter Trail
1403-1440	Henry Wardlaw
1440-1465	James Kennedy (founder of St Salvator's College)
1465-1478	Patrick Graham (created Archbishop 1472)
1478-1497	William Scheves
1497-1504	James Stewart
1504-1513	Alexander Stewart (founder of St Leonard's College, killed at Flodden)
1514-1521	Andrew Forman
1521-1539	James Beaton
1539-1546	David Beaton (assassinated by the Protestants)

1546-1571	John Hamilton (last of the Catholic Archbishops, driven from his See in 1559)
1571-1574	John Douglas
1575-1592	Patrick Adamson
	Episcopacy abolished in 1592. Revived in 1610.
1604-1615	George Gledstanes (existing bishops were allowed to remain in place. Bishop Gledstanes moved to St Andrews from Caithness in 1604).
1615-1638	John Spottiswood
	Episcopacy again abolished in 1638. Revived 1661-89.
1661-1679	James Sharp (murdered at Magus Muir)
1679-1684	Alexander Burnet
1684-1689	Arthur Ross

Table 3: Winners of the Open Championship at St Andrews

Date	Winner	Club/Country
1873	Tom Kidd	St Andrews
1876	Bob Martin	St Andrews
1879	Jamie Anderson	St Andrews
1882	Bob Ferguson	Musselburgh
1885	Bob Martin	St Andrews
1888	Jack Burns	England
1891	Hugh Kirkaldy	St Andrews
1895	J.H.Taylor	England
1900	J.H.Taylor	England
1905	James Braid	England
1910	James Braid	England
1921	Jock Hutchison	USA
1927	Bobby Jones	USA
1933	Densmore Shute	USA
1939	Dick Burton	England
1946	Sam Snead	USA
1955	Peter Thomson	Australia
1957	Bobby Locke	South Africa
1960	Kel Nagle	Australia
1964	Tony Lema	USA
1970	Jack Nicklaus	USA
1978	Jack Nicklaus	USA
1984	Seve Ballesteros	Spain
1990	Nick Faldo	England
1995	John Daly	USA

References

1. Tacitus. See also, *Atlas of Scottish History to 1707*, ed P. McNeill and H. MacQueen (University of Edinburgh, 1996), p.37.
2. R. Lamont-Brown, *The Life and Times of St Andrews* (John Donald, 1989), p.5.
3. *Conversion and Christianity in the Medieval World*, ed B.E. Crawford (University of St Andrews, 1998), p.57.
4. *St Andrews Cathedral* (Historic Scotland, 1993), p.4.
5. Jurek Pütter, *A Feast of Images*, Lectures, 1995.
6. J. Prebble, *The Lion in the North* (Book Club Associates, 1973), p.179.
7. James Grierson, *Delineation of St Andrews* (3rd edn, Tullis, 1838), p.78.
8. Johnson and Boswell, *Tour to the Hebrides*, ed. Chapman, (Oxford University Press, 1924), p.6.
9. Grierson, op. cit, p.78.
10. R.G. Cant, *The University of St Andrews* (St Andrews University Library, 1992), p.141.
11. R. Burnet, *The St Andrews Opens* (John Donald, 1990), p.6.
12. P. Lewis, E.Clark and F.Grieve, *A Round of History* (R&A Golf Club Trust, 1998), p.3.
13. J. Glover, *Golf: A Celebration of 100 years of the Rules of Play* (Macmillan, 1997), p.39.
14. Glover, op. cit., p.10.
15. Lamont-Brown, op. cit., p.72.
16. J.K. Robertson, *About St Andrews and About* (Innes, 1973), p.65.
17. Robertson, op. cit., p.66.
18. D. McRoberts, *The Medieval Church of St Andrews* (Burns, 1976), p.5.
19. McRoberts, op.cit, p.1.
20. McRoberts, op. cit., p.77.
21. Selections from *Scotichronicon*, Walter Bower (ed. D.E.R. Watt) (Mercat Press, 1998).
22. Bower, op. cit, p.92.
23. McRoberts, op. cit., p.101.
24. Bower, op. cit, pp.218-20.
25. *St Andrews Cathedral*, op. cit., p.11.
26. C. Forrest, *Living in St Andrews* (St Andrews University Library, 1996), p.50.
27. Prebble, op. cit., p.177.
28. McRoberts, op. cit., p.109.

29. John Knox, *A Quartercentenary Reappraisal*, ed D. Shaw (Saint Andrew Press), 1975, p.4.
30. McRoberts, op. cit., p.118.
31. Johnson and Boswell, op. cit., p.198.
32. McRoberts. op. cit., p.117.
33. McRoberts op. cit., p.117.
34. P. Yeoman, *Pilgrimage in Medieval Scotland* (Historic Scotland/ Batsford, 1999), p.54.
35. Lamont-Brown, op.cit., p.30.
36. W.T. Linskill, *St Andrews Ghost Stories* (J&G Innes Ltd.)
37. K. Mackie, *Golf at St Andrews* (Aurum Press, 1995), p.104.
38. *Golfing Skeletons in Family History* (Fife Family History Society, 1998), p.15.
39. Burial details from J.K. McCartney, *St Andrews*, and his article in the *Links Trust Yearbook* 1995.
40. Andra Kirkaldy, *Fifty Years of Golf: My Memories* (T. Fisher Unwin, 1921), p.18.
41. Lamont-Brown, op. cit., p.86.
42. Forrest, op. cit., p.31.
43. A.I. Dunlop, *The Life and Times of James Kennedy* (Oliver & Boyd, 1950), p.357.
44. Forrest, op. cit., p.36.
45. Forrest, op. cit., p.33.
46. Forrest, op. cit., p.92.
47. D.W. Lyle, *Shadows of St Andrews Past* (John Donald, 1989), p.22.
48. Lyle, op. cit., p.23.
49. Andra Kirkaldy, op. cit., p.108.
50. Lamont-Brown, op. cit., p.86.
51. C.J. Lyon, *History of St Andrews,* vol 1 (William Tait, 1843), p.27.
52. Jurek Pütter, *The Bishop's Palace* (lecture notes).
53. W. Boulting, *Pope Pius II* (Archibald Constable, 1908), p.56.
54. *St Andrews Castle*, Historic Scotland, 1992, p.2.
55. Bower, op. cit., p.81.
56. J. Herkless and R.K.Hannay, *The Archbishops of St Andrews*, vol 1 (William Blackwood, 1907), pp.1-69.
57. Prebble, op. cit., p.184.
58. Jurek Pütter, *The Bishop's Palace* (lecture notes).
59. Forrest, op. cit., p.49.
60. Lamont Brown, op. cit., p.57.
61. R. Burnet, *An Anecdotal History of the R&A* (1993), p.15.
62. J. Behrend and P. Lewis, *Challenges and Champions* (R&A, 1998) p.42.
63. Jarrett, *St Andrews Golf Links* (Mainstream, 1995), p.126.
64. Burnet, op. cit., p.6.

65. Kirkaldy, op. cit., p.185.
66. Jarrett, op. cit., p.91.
67. From *Golfing Skeletons*, op. cit., pp.10-14.
68. Lewis, Clark and Grieve, op. cit., p.13.
69. J.L.Low, *F.G.Tait A Record* (J.Nisbet, 1988), p.72.
70. Behrend and Lewis, op. cit., p.89.
71. Burnet, op. cit., p.16.
72. Harry Fulford, *Golf's Little Ironies* (Simpkin Marshall Hamilton Kent, 1919).
73. Kirkaldy, op. cit., p.158.
74. Kirkaldy, op. cit., p.158.
 5. Low, op. cit., foreword.
76. Burnet, op. cit., p.112.
77. Burnet, op. cit., p.114-18.
78. Peter Lewis, British Golf Museum (verbal).
79. George Rogers Jr., *The History of Golf in South Carolina in the Late 18th Century*.
80. Golfing Skeletons, op. cit., p.20.
81. McCartney (Links) op. cit., p.92.
82. Behrend and Lewis, op. cit., p.16.
83. Behrend and Lewis, op. cit., p.65.
84. *The Best of Henry Longhurst*, Wilson and Bowden (eds) (Fontana/ Collins, 1979), p.177.
85. Burnet, op. cit., p.108.
86. Kirkaldy, op. cit., p.18.
87. Jarrett, op. cit., p.94.
88. Burnett, op cit., p.72.
89. Charles Roger, *History of St Andrews* (1849, 2nd edn), p.112.
90. Dunlop, op. cit., p.346.
91. Dunlop, op. cit., p.328.
92. R.G. Cant, *The College of St Salvator* (Oliver & Boyd, 1950), p.168.
93. Mabel Irvine, *Sir James Irvine* (Blackwood, 1970), p.120.
94. Bertrand Russell, *A History of Western Philosophy* (Allen & Unwin, 1947), p.145.
95. Herkless and Hannay, op. cit., pp.215-27.
96. Herkless and Hannay op. cit., pp.262-4.
97. Cant, op. cit., pp.36-7.
98. Cant, op. cit., p.37.
99. Cant, op. cit., p.50.
100. Cant, op. cit., p.74.
101. Cant, op. cit., pp.94-5.
102. A.Lang, *St Andrews* (Longmans Green & Co., 1893), p.314.
103. Forrest, op. cit., p.123.

104. Cant, op. cit., p.111.
105. Cant, op. cit., p.118.
106. Cant, op. cit., p.118.
107. Cant, op. cit., p.141.
108. Cant, op. cit., p.116.
109. Twiss and Chennell, *Famous Rectors of St Andrews* (Alvie Publications, 1982), pp.50-8.
110. Twiss, op. cit., pp.60-9.
111. Jurek Pütter (notes).
112. From the *St Andrews Gazette* the forerunner of the *Citizen*.
113. Forrest, op cit., p.42.
114. Forrest, op cit., p.30.
115. Forrest, op cit., pp.13-14.
116. Forrest, op cit., p.22.
117. Forrest, op cit., p.73.
118. R.G. Cant, *The Parish Church of Holy Trinity* (St Andrews, 1992), p.2.
119. Forrest, op cit., pp.22-4.
120. Cant, *Holy Trinity*, op. cit., p.20.
121. Buckroyd, *The Life of James Sharp* (John Donald, 1987), p.107.
122. Buckroyd, op. cit., p.1-2.
123. Buckroyd, op. cit., p.106.
124. Glen, *Illustrious Fife* (Akros Publications, 1998), p.181.
125. Lang, op. cit., p.317.
126. Lang, op. cit., p.326.
127. Lang, op. cit., p.323-4.
128. Lang, op. cit., p.328.
129. Forrest, op. cit., p.196.
130. Lang, op. cit., p.345.
131. Lamont-Brown, op. cit., p.148.
132. Lewis, Clark and Grieve, op. cit., p.7.
133. Lyle, op. cit., p.48.
134. Kirkaldy, op.cit., p.34.
135. R. Mackenzie, *A Wee Nip at the 19th Hole* (Collins Willow, 1997), p.58.
136. Mackenzie, op. cit., p.54.
137. Behrend and Lewis, op. cit., p.126.
138. Mackenzie, op. cit., p.57.
139. Lewis, Clark and Grieve, op. cit., p.3.
140. Burnet, op. cit., p.7.
141. Mackie, op. cit., p.47.
142. Jarrett, op. cit., p.119.
143. Lamont-Brown, op. cit., p.170.

Index

Some other books published by **LUATH** PRESS

LUATH GUIDES TO SCOTLAND

These guides are not your traditional where-to-stay and what-to-eat books. They are companions in the rucksack or car seat, providing the discerning traveller with a blend of fiery opinion and moving description. Here you will find *'that curious pastiche of myths and legend and history that the Scots use to describe their heritage... what battle happened in which glen between which clans; where the Picts sacrificed bulls as recently as the 17th century... A lively counterpoint to the more standard, detached guidebook... Intriguing.'*

THE WASHINGTON POST

These are perfect guides for the discerning visitor or resident to keep close by for reading again and again, written by authors who invite you to share their intimate knowledge and love of the areas covered.

Mull and Iona: Highways and Byways

Peter Macnab

ISBN 0 946487 58 8 PBK £4.95

'The Isle of Mull is of Isles the fairest,
Of ocean's gems 'tis the first and rarest.'

So a local poet described it a hundred years ago, and this recently revised guide to Mull and sacred Iona, the most accessible islands of the Inner Hebrides, takes the reader on a delightful tour of these rare ocean gems, travelling with a native whose unparalleled knowledge and deep feeling for the area unlock the byways of the islands in all their natural beauty.

South West Scotland

Tom Atkinson

ISBN 0 946487 04 9 PBK £4.95

This descriptive guide to the magical country of Robert Burns covers Kyle, Carrick, Galloway, Dumfriesshire, Kirkcudbrightshire and Wigtownshire. Hills, unknown moors and unspoiled beaches grace a land steeped in history and legend and portrayed with affection and deep delight.

An essential book for the visitor who yearns to feel at home in this land of peace and grandeur.

The West Highlands: The Lonely Lands

Tom Atkinson

ISBN 0 946487 56 1 PBK £4.95

A guide to Inveraray, Glencoe, Loch Awe, Loch

Lomond, Cowal, the Kyles of Bute and all of central Argyll written with insight, sympathy and loving detail. Once Atkinson has taken you there, these lands can never feel lonely. 'I have sought to make the complex simple, the beautiful accessible and the strange familiar,' he writes, and indeed he brings to the land a knowledge and affection only accessible to someone with intimate knowledge of the area.

A must for travellers and natives who want to delve beneath the surface.

'Highly personal and somewhat quirky... steeped in the lore of Scotland.'
THE WASHINGTON POST

The Northern Highlands: The Empty Lands

Tom Atkinson

ISBN 0 946487 55 3 PBK £4.95

The Highlands of Scotland from Ullapool to Bettyhill and Bonar Bridge to John O' Groats are landscapes of myth and legend, 'empty of people, but of nothing else that brings delight to any tired soul,' writes Atkinson. This highly personal guide describes Highland history and landscape with love, compassion and above all sheer magic.

Essential reading for anyone who has dreamed of the Highlands.

The North West Highlands: Roads to the Isles

Tom Atkinson

ISBN 0 946487 54 5 PBK £4.95

Ardnamurchan, Morvern, Morar, Moidart and the west coast to Ullapool are included in this guide to the Far West and Far North of Scotland. An unspoiled land of mountains, lochs and silver sands is brought to the walker's toe-tips (and to the reader's fingertips) in this stark, serene and evocative account of town, country and legend.

For any visitor to this Highland wonderland, Queen Victoria's favourite place on earth.

POETRY

Poems to be read aloud
Collected and with an introduction by
Tom Atkinson
ISBN 0 946487 00 6 PBK £5.00

Scots Poems to be Read Aloud
Collectit an wi an innin by
Stuart McHardy
ISBN 0 946487 81 2 PBK £5.00

Men & Beasts
Valerie Gillies amd Rebecca Marr
ISBN 0 946487 92 8 PBK £15.00

The Luath Burns Companion
John Cairney
ISBN 1 84282 000 1 PBK £10.00

'Nothing but Heather!'
Gerry Cambridge
ISBN 0 946487 49 9 PBK £15.00

FICTION

The Strange Case of R L Stevenson
Richard Woodhead
ISBN 0 946487 86 3 HBK £16.99

The Bannockburn Years
William Scott
ISBN 0 946487 34 0 PBK £7.95

But n Ben A-Go-Go
Matthew Fitt
ISBN 0 946487 82 0 HBK £10.99

The Great Melnikov
Hugh MacLachlan
ISBN 0 946487 42 1 PBK £7.95

FOLKLORE

Scotland: Myth Legend & Folklore
Stuart McHardy
ISBN 0 946487 69 3 PBK £7.99

Luath Storyteller: Highland Myths & Legends
George W Macpherson
ISBN 1 84282 003 6 PBK £5.00

Tall Tales from an Island
Peter Macnab
ISBN 0 946487 07 3 PBK £8.99

Tales from the North Coast
Alan Temperley
ISBN 0 946487 18 9 PBK £8.99

ON THE TRAIL OF

On the Trail of Mary Queen of Scots
J. Keith Cheetham
ISBN 0 946487 50 2 PBK £7.99

On the Trail of William Wallace
David R. Ross
ISBN 0 946487 47 2 PBK £7.99

On the Trail of Robert Burns
John Cairney
ISBN 0 946487 51 0 PBK £7.99

On the Trail of Bonnie Prince Charlie
David R. Ross
ISBN 0 946487 68 5 PBK £7.99

On the Trail of Queen Victoria in the Highlands
Ian R. Mitchell
ISBN 0 946487 79 0 PBK £7.99

On the Trail of Robert the Bruce
David R. Ross
ISBN 0 946487 52 9 PBK £7.99

On the Trail of Robert Service
GW Lockhart
ISBN 0 946487 24 3 PBK £7.99

On the Trail of the Pilgrim Fathers
J. Keith Cheetham
ISBN 0 946487 83 9 PBK £7.99

WALK WITH LUATH

The Joy of Hillwalking
Ralph Storer
ISBN 0 946487 28 6 PBK £7.50

Scotland's Mountains before the Mountaineers
Ian R. Mitchell
ISBN 0 946487 39 1 PBK £9.99

LUATH WALKING GUIDES

Walks in the Cairngorms
Ernest Cross
ISBN 0 946487 09 X PBK £4.95

Short Walks in the Cairngorms
Ernest Cross
ISBN 0 946487 23 5 PBK £4.95

HISTORY

Reportage Scotland: History in the Making
Louise Yeoman
ISBN 0 946487 61 8 PBK £9.99

Old Scotland New Scotland
Jeff Fallow
ISBN 0 946487 40 5 PBK £6.99

**Notes from the North
Incorporating a Brief History of the
Scots and the English**
Emma Wood
ISBN 0 946487 46 4 PBK £8.99

**Some Assembly Required: behind the
scenes at the rebirth of the Scottish
Parliament**
David Shepherd
ISBN 0 946487 84 7 PBK £7.99

Blind Harry's Wallace
William Hamilton of Gilbertfield
introduced by Elspeth King
ISBN 0 946487 43 X HBK £15.00
ISBN 0 946487 33 2 PBK £8.99

Edinburgh's Historic Mile
Duncan Priddle
ISBN 0 946487 97 9 PBK £2.99

A Word for Scotland
Jack Campbell
foreword by Magnus Magnusson
ISBN 0 946487 48 0 PBK £12.99

SOCIAL HISTORY

Shale Voices
Alistair Findlay
foreword by Tam Dalyell MP
ISBN 0 946487 63 4 PBK £10.99
ISBN 0 946487 78 2 HBK £17.99

Crofting Years
Francis Thompson
ISBN 0 946487 06 5 PBK £6.95

BIOGRAPHY

**Tobermory Teuchter: a first-hand
account of life on Mull in the early
years of the 20th century**
Peter Macnab
ISBN 0 946487 41 3 PBK £7.99

The Last Lighthouse
Sharma Kraustopf
ISBN 0 946487 96 0 PBK £7.99

Bare Feet & Tackety Boots
Archie Cameron
ISBN 0 946487 17 0 PBK £7.95

Come Dungeons Dark
John Taylor Caldwell
ISBN 0 946487 19 7 PBK £6.95

MUSIC AND DANCE

Highland Balls & Village Halls
GW Lockhart
ISBN 0 946487 12 X PBK £6.95

**Fiddles & Folk: a celebration of the
re-emergence of Scotland's musical
heritage**
GW Lockhart
ISBN 0 946487 38 3 PBK £7.95

TRAVEL

Edinburgh & Leith Pub Guide
Stuart McHardy
ISBN 0 946487 80 4 PBK £4.99

Die kleine Schottlandfibel
Hans-Walter Arends
ISBN 0 946487 89 8 PBK £8.99

SPORT

**Over the Top with the Tartan Army
(Active Service 1992-97)**
Andrew McArthur
ISBN 0 946487 45 6 PBK £7.99

Ski & Snowboard Scotland
Hilary Parke
ISBN 0 946487 35 9 PBK £6.99

NATURAL WORLD

**Wild Lives: Otters – On the Swirl of the
Tide**
Bridget MacCaskill
ISBN 0 946487 67 7 PBK £9.99

Wild Lives: Foxes – The Blood is Wild
Bridget MacCaskill
ISBN 0 946487 71 5 PBK £9.99

**Wild Scotland: The essential guide to
finding the best of natural Scotland**
James McCarthy
Photography by Laurie Campbell
ISBN 0 946487 37 5 PBK £7.50

**Scotland Land and People
An Inhabited Solitude**
James McCarthy
ISBN 0 946487 57 X PBK £7.99

The Highland Geology Trail
John L Roberts
ISBN 0 946487 36 7 PBK £4.99

Rum: Nature's Island
Magnus Magnusson
ISBN 0 946487 32 4 PBK £7.95

Red Sky at Night
John Barrington
ISBN 0 946487 60 X PBK £8.99

Luath Press Limited
committed to publishing well written books worth reading

LUATH PRESS takes its name from Robert Burns, whose little collie Luath (*Gael.,* swift or nimble) tripped up Jean Armour at a wedding and gave him the chance to speak to the woman who was to be his wife and the abiding love of his life. Burns called one of *The Twa Dogs* Luath after Cuchullin's hunting dog in *Ossian's Fingal*. Luath Press grew up in the heart of Burns country, and now resides a few steps up the road from Burns' first lodgings in Edinburgh's Royal Mile.
Luath offers you distinctive writing with a hint of unexpected pleasures.

Most UK and US bookshops either carry our books in stock or can order them for you. To order direct from us, please send a £sterling cheque, postal order, international money order or your credit card details (number, address of cardholder and expiry date) to us at the address below. Please add post and packing as follows: UK – £1.00 per delivery address; overseas surface mail – £2.50 per delivery address; overseas airmail – £3.50 for the first book to each delivery address, plus £1.00 for each additional book by airmail to the same address. If your order is a gift, we will happily enclose your card or message at no extra charge.

Luath Press Limited
543/2 Castlehill
The Royal Mile
Edinburgh EH1 2ND
Scotland
Telephone: 0131 225 4326 (24 hours)
Fax: 0131 225 4324
email: gavin.macdougall@luath.co.uk
Website: www.luath.co.uk